ROCK
THE
DANCE
FLOOR!

The proven five-step
formula for total
DJing success

PHIL MORSE

Praise

"Phil Morse is on a lifelong mission not only to get more people into the world of DJing, but to make sure they do so in the right way. I've read and watched his work over many years, and have always found his approach to be both accessible *and* comprehensive - a rare quality indeed. With this new book he breaks down the process of learning to DJ into simple steps any music fan could take."

Mojaxx, DJ City

"Phil just delivers the goods when it comes to DJ education - and he does it in a way that's very comprehensible, not pretentious or preachy. There are many ways of succeeding as a DJ nowadays, but the competition is fierce, so you gotta be versatile and always stay on top of your game. This is where the advice of such an experienced DJ tutor with a background in journalism and club promoting becomes invaluable."

Karsten Hainmueller, Traktor

"An extremely thorough and comprehensive look at the art of DJing. If you can't rock a party after reading this book and using the classic techniques and cool tricks it presents, you should probably try something else!"

Baptiste Grange, Serato

"*Rock The Dancefloor!* is a great asset for any DJ looking at how to get ahead in the DJing industry. The book contains a wealth of knowledge and practical information, that will help boost any DJ's career. Phil has amassed a veritable fount of knowledge from his time as a DJ and also as founder of Digital DJ Tips. His five-step system is an easy to follow guide for both beginners and experienced DJs. A great read whilst taking five from the day to day, or travelling from gig to gig."

Mick Wilson, DJ Mag

"There aren't many experienced, intelligent and sober people in this game, so when one of them commits to writing a full no-stone-unturned guide to DJing, you know it's an essential purchase!"

Rik Parkinson, Pioneer DJ

"If you are starting out as a DJ then this book is a no-brainer. If you've been a DJ for years then this book is a no-brainer! A 360° insight into the world of a DJ from instruction to getting yourself gigs and everything in-between."

Mark Walsh, Marked Events (BPM Pro Show Organisers)

"Phil from Digital DJ Tips has just created *the* one-stop resource for DJs that taps into thousands of hours of real life, real industry and real time DJ experience. From choice of equipment, music preparation and mixing techniques, right through to playing out in different scenarios and how to best promote yourself, securing a long-term career path in this most aspiring and creative of industries, this guide has it all and more. This is your fast-track solution to removing all the hurdles that beset any DJ starting their journey – just add your creativity, imagination and dreams and Phil will provide the rest!"

Paul "Tinman" Dakeyne, producer/remixer

"I wish there had been a book like this when I started DJing. It's the essential How-To guide for any new DJ starting out, and has a lot to teach old dogs like me, too!"

David Dunne, club DJ, radio presenter and former head of music at MTV

"Phil really knows his stuff. His experience as a DJ, his success with Digital DJ Tips and, most importantly, his compassion in helping DJs of any level makes this a must-read for anyone interested in playing music for others."

Constantin Koehncke, Native Instruments

RƎTHINK PRESS

First published in Great Britain 2016
by Rethink Press (www.rethinkpress.com)

Contents

For Tony

Introduction

This book will teach you how to be a great DJ. Whether you want to land a dream gig in your favourite nightclub, play at that cool lounge bar in your town, set up as a mobile DJ, or just provide the music at parties for friends and family, everything you need to know is within these pages.

You wouldn't be alone in wanting to learn this. In an age where DJs are just as important as rock stars, it's not surprising that more people than ever are getting interested in the art and science of spinning tunes. Nobody ever forgets their first big dancefloor experience, or the DJ who provided it. Who wouldn't want to be in his or her shoes, at one with the crowd, gratefully receiving all that adoration and praise from a packed dancefloor?

As with so many things, DJing has been utterly transformed by the arrival of the digital age. Record shops largely no longer exist, having been replaced by online download stores and streaming music websites. For minimal outlay, you can buy DJ gear small enough to fit in your desk drawer that - working in tandem with your laptop - does so much more than the old-fashioned turntables and mixers of only a generation ago, and at a fraction of the cost. This has radically altered how today's DJs learn the craft, and given them a much wider choice of venues to play in - beach bars, cafes, and other smaller establishments, which could never fit traditional gear into their premises, happily welcome the new breed of 'digital DJs'. The ways DJs share their work, gather a fan base and promote themselves have also completely changed in just a few short years.

Yet as the barriers to entry have lowered, making it sometimes feel like everyone is (or says they are) a DJ, paradoxically, the path to becoming a great DJ has become less clear. While learning the technical skills of DJing on old-fashioned equipment could be tricky, at least the route was clear. Nowadays, there is a hugely confusing choice of equipment, software, music file formats, and features that, at the same time as making digital DJing hugely exciting, has made it at best, puzzling, and at worse, a potentially expensive minefield for inexperienced DJs. What skills are you meant to be learning? What shortcuts is it OK to take? How will you know when you're good enough to play in public? How exactly are you meant to stand out and get ahead when everyone is a DJ?

That's why I wrote this book. As a DJ myself for over a quarter of a century, with a career that's taken me from the bars and clubs of my native Manchester to no lesser a venue than Privilege in Ibiza, the biggest club in the world, I've learned a thing or two about what it takes to achieve DJing success. As a self-proclaimed geek, too, I was one of the first to adopt digital DJing, back in 2004. The magazine I wrote for, *iDJ*, started passing the very earliest digital DJ controllers to me to review, because I was the only person who knew how they worked. I immediately saw the potential of these new devices to revolutionise the world of DJing, which over the next five years they duly did, just as I'd predicted. Taking my skills from learning to DJ 'the old way' and applying them to the problems I could see the new generation of DJs having with this type of equipment and software, I founded Digital DJ Tips, which has gone on to become the world's biggest online DJ school, training tens of thousands of DJs in more than fifty countries. This book is the result of my experiences both as a DJ and in training others.

THE FIVE STEPS OF DJING SUCCESS

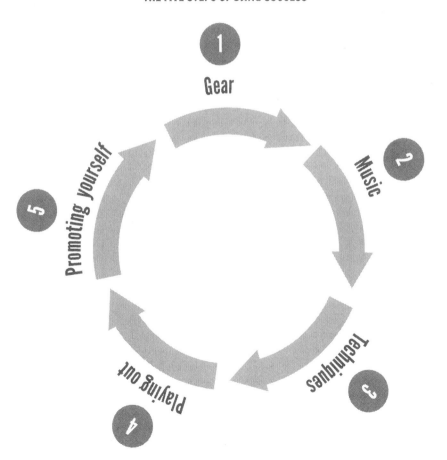

The book is divided into five core steps: Gear, Music, Techniques, Playing Out, and Promoting Yourself. It takes you logically, clearly and practically through the minefield, helping you to find the best tunes, master your equipment, practise effectively, smash it when you play your first gig, and then do all the things you need to do to keep the bookings rolling in. Whether you're a complete beginner, a bedroom DJ, a semi-pro, an experienced DJ returning to the game and curious about all this new technology, or even a musician or music producer wanting to add DJing to your skills and further your career, this book has been designed for you.

Whatever your type of music and wherever in the world you are, the truth is that, as a modern DJ, your skills need to be universal and transferrable. A mobile DJ might get the chance to play a club gig, and have to change their music radically as a result; a bedroom DJ may aspire to play a local festival, and need to know how to use the equipment provided instead of their own set-up; an underground DJ may be cajoled into playing a family member's wedding, and need to learn a whole new way of filling dancefloors.

In these modern times, the best DJs can not only play on any type of gear, but can put their minds to playing any type of DJ set too. Yet so much remains the same. Every night, in every big town and city in the world, countless DJs are stepping up to fill dancefloors and help people dance the night away. All have the chance to find great new music and be the first to play it to their audiences. When you reduce it to its core, DJing is still about playing the right music for the people in front of you, right now. This book will help you to become the type of DJ who's fit and able to do that in these exciting times.

Step One: Gear

In this first step of the process, we'll cover all things 'gear'. I'll start by showing you the various parts that all DJ set-ups share in common, so you can see past the marketing hype and 'shiny new thing' syndrome and be sure about what you really need. You'll learn why nowadays it's almost always necessary to have a DJ laptop (even if you want to DJ on the one hand with old-fashioned turntables, or on the other using just a tablet), and we'll look at what software you'll need to have for your laptop. With your head aligned to what's really important and the computer side of it taken care of, I'll talk you through your hardware choices - not only the DJ gear itself, but all the accessories and extras you'll need to complete your set-up. And finally, I'll show you how to set everything up properly for smooth, trouble-free DJing.

Digital DJ Tips produces two free annually updated guides, covering all the latest DJ gear and software. Download your copies of each today from: http://www.digitaldjtips.com/gearguide

Understanding DJ Gear

Introduction

Before you can have any confidence at all about making the right choices when it comes to spending the (sometimes large) sums of money needed to buy a DJ set-up, you need a good understanding of what DJ gear does. While just a few years ago, buying the gear was easy, albeit rather expensive (you bought two specialist turntables and a 'mixer' – the bit that sat between them and allowed you to blend the music the turntables were playing – plus some speakers and headphones, and you were done), today the choice out there is mind-boggling.

From everything-in-one-box systems to club-style DJ CD decks and mixers, to DJ software that runs on your laptop (and can work with or without various extra gadgets plugged in), to digital vinyl systems ('DVS'), to DJ apps for your tablet (or even your phone)…spend a cursory half hour browsing 'DJ set-up' online and you'd be forgiven for walking away twice as confused as when you started.

But if you're to start your new DJing hobby or career off on the right foot, and avoid a potentially expensive mistake or series of mistakes, you need to think like a pro. Luckily, I'm here to show you what the pros see when they assess *any* DJ set-up to help you cut through the marketing speak and avoid the shiny new thing trap that can lead to expensive, frustrating errors.

Ah, that shiny new thing syndrome. You know what I mean: being seduced by the latest and the greatest, this year's 'must have' this or that. We see people fall into this trap all the time at Digital DJ Tips, where we train thousands of people a year to DJ. It is always beginners, never pros, who suffer from this, and we usually diagnose it when we receive something like this in our inbox:

> *Hi! I've been DJing for a bit, but I'm struggling to get any better. Can you help? I've realised that my current set-up is a bit limited and I probably made a mistake when I bought it. I really should have bought something better first time around. Should I upgrade? In fact, there's something coming out next year that actually seems to have everything I need on it, and also has some stuff I hadn't thought of but that looks great. Truth is, I don't know what to do! Do I trade in my gear for something else, or wait a year and then buy the amazing new gear that's just around the corner? Either way I've got to do something, as my DJing is stalling right now…*

Whenever I get a letter, email or forum comment like that, I patiently explain two things. Firstly, you can do more DJing on a cheap or free DJ app on your mobile phone today than the very best DJ systems could achieve just a decade or so ago, so unless you're a very advanced DJ, there's little to be gained from putting a hole in your wallet to chop and change your set-up. And secondly, if your DJing is stalling, the issue is never – listen to me – *never* your gear. It is *always* what you're doing (or not doing) with that gear.

We'll get on to the second point a little later, but the first point is important for now. Whatever you choose to DJ on (and by the end of this step you'll know for sure what you'll need), it's going to be OK. As long as you follow the advice here, I guarantee that you'll be confident in your first DJ gear purchase, and be certain that you're equipping yourself with everything you need to learn to DJ quickly and effectively.

How pros see DJ set-ups

So to begin to understand what's really going on in a DJ system - *any* DJ system - let's pretend we're in the shoes of a pro DJ. Not any pro DJ, but a pro DJ who has just been asked whether he can play a DJ set on a completely unfamiliar set-up in ten minutes' time. Our hero has clearly got no time to worry about the amazing must have features of this fantastic but totally alien DJ system. After all, he has got just a few minutes to get ready and then he's expected to perform.

So what does he look for in order to say yes or no to this request? What parts does he have to identify in order to decide if this strange DJ set-up has got what it takes for him to deliver the goods? There are just four things. Here they are:

Two independent music sources. In order for a DJ to play music continuously, he needs two music sources, so when he is playing a piece of music to his audience using one of those sources, he can prepare the next piece of music using the other. This is so he can make a gapless transition between the two tracks when the time is right. A DJ's music sources are commonly called his or her 'decks'. Our DJ is going to want to know whether the format he has his music in can be played on whatever decks are available (for instance, it'd be pointless trying to play digital music files if all he's got for decks are a pair of old record players…).

A way of switching between the decks. There's not much point having two ways of playing music without being able to switch between them, and preferably do a bit more than that, such as 'fading' the music sources together (which is why the controls used to do this are typically called 'faders'). Otherwise, our DJ would need a separate amplifier and speaker system for each source, which would be crazy. So clearly a 'mixer' (to give this part of any DJ set-up its proper title) is a must-have.

A way of getting the music to the audience. Once our hero has his music sources identified and a way of blending them together, he needs to get that output from the mixer to the audience. So the next step in the equation is to identify the loudspeakers and the amplification system necessary to make the music loud enough, so that whether there are ten or 10,000 people ready to enjoy the DJ set, they can all hear it well. Our DJ is going to want to know that the speaker system is fit for purpose and how to control it.

A way of listening to stuff the audience isn't hearing. Typically via a pair of headphones, our pro DJ definitely needs a way of listening to the music source or sources that the audience *isn't* currently hearing. DJs need this function for several reasons: for instance, in order to preview the next track to see if it's suitable, to 'cue' the track up (to get it to the right point to start it playing when the time is right), or to adjust its levels so that when it's time to play it through the loudspeakers, it sounds just as good as the track currently playing. That's why the ability to monitor something different from what the audience is hearing is essential.

And that's it. At its heart, a DJ system simply needs to have these four things. Once our pro has worked this through, he will know whether it's possible to play on the gear in front of him or not. Indeed, a typical pro DJ faced with any unfamiliar set-up will work out the above in minutes, if not seconds. The internal dialogue will go something like this:

OK, let's turn everything down first so we don't have any loud surprises. Right, now how do I get my music playing? Ah right, here. Where do I plug my headphones in? Right, there! Let's hit play…I can see the meters working, it's coming through. The other deck? Yup, that's playing too. Now, where are my headphones' volume and selector? Great. Master volume? Are the amps on? Let's turn it up a bit. There we go! Yup, that sounds good, I reckon this will be loud enough when we crank things up. OK, all set! Now, where's the audience? I'll work everything else out as I go along…

As you work through the following chapters in this section of the book, I'll be explaining your options in terms of these four parts, because it will help you to understand perfectly well the otherwise bewildering range of choices out there. By the end of the section, you'll have all the information you need to make a good choice when it comes to equipping yourself with a DJ set-up of your own.

Keep your choice of gear in context

Before we get stuck in, I want to return to the second point that I make to any DJ who writes to me frustrated, blaming their gear for their lack of progress. While a good DJ will be able to play on *every* DJ set-up (as long as it has the four basic elements), a bad DJ will struggle to play on *any* DJ set-up.

The truth is that DJing isn't about the gear, any more than photography is about the camera or writing is about the pen you hold. These things are all just tools of the trade, and while of course they have an influence on what is and isn't possible, at the end of the day it's what you do with them that counts. Later on in this book you'll learn about all the various things you need to be a great DJ, but past a pretty early point, the gear isn't one of them.

Read this step well, choose wisely, then forget about your gear. We'll have more important things to concern ourselves with from step two onwards, I promise you. Indeed, my students tell me that the beauty of the way I teach DJing is that by the end of one of our courses they feel confident that they'll be able to pick up the skills on *any* DJ gear, not just the particular DJ set-up they have bought for themselves.

However, one thing is certain: even the best DJs can't play with *nothing*. So let's start at a place you may be surprised by, but which actually, as you'll see, makes perfect sense: your computer.

How To Choose Your DJ Laptop

Introduction

'Why do I need a DJ laptop anyway?'

It's a good question, because while 'laptop DJing' (having a laptop right there with you when you DJ) is pretty common nowadays, it's by no means the only way of DJing. Maybe you just want to use CDs, which is another common way of DJing. Or maybe you're fancying DJing from your iPad. Or maybe you've spotted a 'no computer required' DJ system, using USB pens or drives to hold your music that you plug into it, and you fancy DJing in a manner similar to that.

You still need a laptop.

Or, to be more accurate, you still need a computer. And let's face it, for most people nowadays, 'computer' means 'laptop'. (If you're adamant that, come what may, you are never, ever going to take your laptop DJing with you, then by all means use a desktop computer instead, but for the rest of this chapter, I'm going to say 'laptop'.)

So why do you need one? In short, in order to prepare your music for DJing with. Because unless you intend only to play vinyl, using old-fashioned record decks, your music is going to be digital, and that means you need a laptop to deal with it. Even if you want to play CDs and just CDs, you're going to need to obtain music digitally in order to burn your own, which means you'll need a computer (and one with a CD burner, too - something that's not standard nowadays).

At the very least, you'll be using your laptop for logging in to online music stores to purchase tracks, which you'll then download, organise, and prepare for DJing with, even if you then transfer that music to CD or USB drive to insert into your DJ gear or export it to your iOS or Android device to DJ from thereafter. And if this is genuinely all you think you're going to be doing with your laptop, the good news is just about any old one will do as the work you're going to have it doing isn't 'mission critical' (i.e. if it lets you down, you won't have 500 people on a dancefloor to answer to).

But if, like many DJs, you choose to do your actual DJing using DJ software, your laptop will stay with you all the way, running that software as you do your thing. In this instance, depending on the kind of DJ gear you're using (if any; it is possible to DJ from a laptop on its own), your laptop acts as your decks and sometimes your mixer too (and your music library, to boot). Sure, you may have DJ hardware plugged in to offer you something more ergonomic than the computer keyboard, but make no mistake, it's the laptop that's doing all the work. So you're going to have to pay a bit more attention to this vital part of your set-up.

Should I buy a new laptop or use the one I've got?

The good news is that if you already own a laptop and you bought it within the last five years, it will almost certainly be good enough to get going with. All modern laptops can run the software needed for anything a DJ is likely to want to do, so in reality it's likely any laptop you own will be able to be pressed right into service as you learn to DJ. If in doubt, every DJ software manufacturer has a page on their website listing the minimum specifications needed for their software to work, so check before you buy.

When it's time to buy a laptop for DJing with, though, there are a number of considerations, some of which might not be what you expect. Here they are:

Get something sturdy. DJ laptops tend to have rough lives. They can get knocked and bumped, stuff spilled on them, hot and damp in sweaty clubs and cold and damp in the boots of cars. And they really need to keep going, because a failed laptop mid-gig is not fun. So something sturdy and well-built is important.

Get something with a big, clear screen. Depending on your eyesight, buying anything with a screen smaller than thirteen inches is likely to be an error. DJ software is notoriously busy, and trying to keep an eye on it on a smaller screen is difficult. Don't just consider the screen size, but consider the resolution, too. If you have bad eyesight, you may find a large screen set to a relatively low resolution suits you better than a smaller screen with a high resolution. And consider the brightness of the screen, especially if you plan to do any daytime DJing, where the sun can quickly turn a dim screen into a practically invisible one.

Get something with enough USB sockets. DJs tend to want to plug things into their laptops, like DJ controllers, audio interfaces, mobile phones (to charge them while gigging), or USB drives. Some DJ set-ups may need you to have two or even three USB sockets just to get up to speed. And you never know how your needs are going to change. Two USB sockets is an absolute minimum; three is better. It is possible to buy USB hubs (go for a powered one) which can expand the number of USB sockets you have while keeping everything reliable as you plug more and more gear in, but it's best to have at least the number you think you'll need in the first place.

Make sure you have enough memory and hard disk space, and go for SSD if you can. Memory will make your DJ software zip along, with faster loading and processing times and smoother running when you're DJing. As far as your hard drive goes, not only are solid state drives, or SSDs, significantly faster than traditional hard disk drives (HDDs), but, since they have no moving parts, they are also more reliable – an important consideration in the DJ booth (see 'Get something sturdy' above). If you're looking for numbers, 8GB of memory and 256GB of hard disk space as a minimum would be a good start; some professional mobile DJs, who need huge music collections in order to fulfil all types of weird and wonderful audience requests, have much bigger hard disks.

Mac or Windows?

This is a debate that rumbles on and on and will probably never be definitively won by either side. The truth is that both platforms can do the job well, and both can let you down. Because DJing is such a mission critical application, and because Macs have a great track record of reliability, DJs have taken to Macs in their droves, knowing they are likely to do the job without a grumble. But even so, among 10,000 readers of Digital DJ Tips who took part in a recent survey, users were still divided right down the middle on this one.

If you can afford it, you may choose to go for a Mac, but if you want to use a Windows computer for whatever reason (can't afford a Mac, already own a Windows device, prefer Windows to Mac OS), don't be put off. A good Windows laptop will serve you just as well, and you'll get the same spec for slightly less money. But what is true is that there are many cheap Windows laptops available which are awful, not because they're running Windows, but simply because they're made of cheap parts. They break down easily, have poor screens, and are too delicate for a life on the road. There's no such thing as a cheap Mac, something that Apple detractors will gleefully point out to those whom they see as paying a premium for the name.

But to go back to where we started, while you're learning to DJ in your bedroom, who cares? If it runs the software, use whatever you've got. There's plenty of time to worry about Mac vs Windows when it's time to buy something new. Actually, what's far more important than the laptop brand is the type of DJ software you choose to run on it. That's what we'll cover in the next chapter.

Choosing Your DJ Software

Introduction

Always consider what DJ software you want to use before you choose your DJ hardware. When you buy a piece of DJ hardware, it comes with the software you need to make it work, so there will typically be a download link for you to go to online and get the software. There will also be instructions for any other pieces of software you may need to get your DJ hardware working (such as 'drivers', which are often necessary if you're using a Windows laptop).

But just as you may replace your laptop many times throughout your lifetime yet you'll probably stick to one platform (i.e. Mac or Windows) due to the learning curve of changing from one to the other, the same is true of DJ software. While you may graduate from a cheap beginner's DJ controller when you start your hobby to using pro gear once you get good at it, you'll be better off sticking to one brand of DJ software throughout. As well as the unnecessary learning curve should you switch programs with DJ software, you also end up doing an awful lot of work on your music over the years and it is hard to bring that with you from one type to the next. That's why we're talking about the software before we talk about the hardware. Get this decision right early on and you won't regret your choice.

But how do you choose?

The big names in DJ software

The main DJ software titles are Serato DJ, Traktor Pro, Virtual DJ and Rekordbox DJ. These programs have lots in common, but they also have differences, some of which are vital. What they've got in common is that they all give you virtual decks (to play your music on), a virtual mixer (to blend your music with), and integration with DJ hardware.

Now let's look at what differentiates them:

Traktor Pro

Traktor Pro comes from a company called Native Instruments, which also makes DJ hardware as well as being big in the music production hardware and software market. That makes Traktor a strong contender if you already produce, or intend to produce, electronic music yourself, because you'll find some interesting producer-friendly features and integrations. It is heavily biased towards electronic music in the way that it works, though, so not the best choice if you intend to play a broader selection of music in your DJ sets.

Serato DJ

While Native Instruments, which makes Traktor, also manufactures hardware, Serato doesn't. Instead, the company tightly integrates its software with a wide range of licensed hardware from third-party companies. Serato DJ is a mature and stable platform, and works well with all types of music, although it's always been particularly loved by scratch DJs. Serato DJ is a good choice if you want to use music videos or visuals in your performances, as it has a good video plug-in that can be purchased in-app.

Virtual DJ

Beloved of mobile DJs for its versatility (it works with just about any hardware, whether officially approved or not), Virtual DJ isn't quite as polished as Serato, but offers much the same feature set, including video – only this time the video facility is built-in. Virtual DJ has been around a long time and picked up a lot of fans, though it has (perhaps unfairly) never quite garnered the same respect as its competitors, possibly due to nothing more than its 'virtual' name wrongly implying it is somehow apart from 'real' DJing.

Rekordbox DJ (and Rekordbox)

Rekordbox DJ comes from Pioneer DJ, one of the biggest names in DJ hardware and the name you're most likely to see in DJ booths across the world. Much newer than the three programs above, Rekordbox DJ is in fact a paid-for plug-in for the (free) Rekordbox program. Rekordbox is used by DJs to prepare their music in order to transfer it to USB drive to play using compatible Pioneer pro DJ booth gear without a laptop. Rekordbox DJ extends Rekordbox so the program can be used as a fully fledged DJ program for laptop DJing, like the three other DJ apps listed above. Like Serato DJ and Virtual DJ, it also has a video option.

How to choose your DJ software

In order to decide which platform is right for you, I suggest you do at least two of the following things:

Ask your DJ friends what they use. If you know anyone who DJs, get their advice. They'll know much more about what's used in your area than I possibly can, and may even be able to show you their software so you can get a feel for it.

Find out what DJs are using in your local venues - especially those you feel you may want to play in as you progress with your DJing. If you turn up early enough you may be able to ask the resident DJ, or try peeking into the DJ booth to see their laptop screen. Alternatively, hit them up on social media and ask.

Browse around the company websites. Many let you download a trial version of the software to get a feel for it, and they also have demo videos of features, pages showing you the hardware that works with their software, and other content to help you make your mind up.

While you should start to think about your DJ software before your hardware, to an extent you need to decide both at the same time. So once you've done the above and are starting to get a feel for software you like and don't like, read the next chapter on DJ gear to understand a bit more about your choices there too. Then, armed with that knowledge, take another look at your software shortlist alongside hardware that you're interested in and see if one particular system jumps out at you - it should by that point.

A word about 'cut-down' DJ software

Often, bundled with DJ hardware, you'll see versions of some of the above programs labelled 'Intro', 'Home', 'Lite', 'Limited Edition', or 'LE'. All of these things mean the same thing: the version you're getting isn't the real deal.

Such software is a little bit like the cheap batteries you sometimes get when you buy electrical gear: designed to get you going, but you'll want to get the real thing pretty quickly. You may find that these cut-down versions won't let you record your DJ sets, or won't work with other hardware, or have some other essential features frustratingly disabled. That's not to say you can't get by on these versions for a while; just factor in the cost of upgrading to the real deal at some point down the line.

So once you have your laptop and you've decided what software route you want to go down, the next step is to decide what DJ hardware you need. We'll look at that in the next chapter.

How To Choose Your DJ Gear

Introduction

The DJ gear you choose is going to depend largely on your budget, and on how seriously you think you're going to take your new hobby (or career). The good news is that nowadays pretty much everything, from cheap smartphone DJ apps to DJ controllers (all-in-one boxes, just add laptop...) to pro set-ups costing many thousands, has got what it takes for you to learn to DJ on it.

In a way, though, that's also the bad news. Whereas in the past, choosing your DJ gear was easy (two record decks and a mixer, of which the choice was severely limited, even when compared to just that single category today), nowadays there are half a dozen different ways of DJing and scores of manufacturers and models to wade through to make your choice.

In this chapter, I'm going to talk through the main types of system. When read alongside the software chapter that preceded it, this chapter will help you decide what to go for.

Types of DJ gear

DJ controllers

*The Pioneer DDJ-SX2, a modern DJ controller that,
in this case, controls Serato DJ software.*

Nowadays, DJ controllers (sometimes referred to as 'Midi controllers') are by far the most popular way for new DJs to get started. A DJ controller is a single box that contains controls for two or more decks, a mixer, various other periphery functions, plus usually an audio interface which sends audio to both your headphones and your amplifier and speakers.

Plug your DJ controller into the laptop on which your DJ software is running and your digital music files are stored, and *voila*! You've got a full DJ system. (Note that such DJ controllers sometimes work with tablets and even smartphones, although laptops are still the preferred computer choice among DJs.)

DJ controllers are great value for money, generally much more portable than traditional DJ gear and thus practical, and are limited only by the sophistication of the software they control, making them exciting to use. On the downside, they are not universally accepted in DJ booths, from both a practical point of view (there's often little room for extra equipment) and because of what seems to be a logical objection of venue owners and managers ('We've got perfectly good DJ gear fitted here already, so why don't you just use that?').

While most DJ controllers still require you to take your laptop along with you for the software to run on, some models work slightly differently, letting you prepare your music using a laptop at home, export the finished set list or library to a USB drive, and plug that directly in when it's time to perform. This alleviates the need to take your computer along with you and mimics the way much more expensive pro DJ gear works.

Digital vinyl systems (DVS)

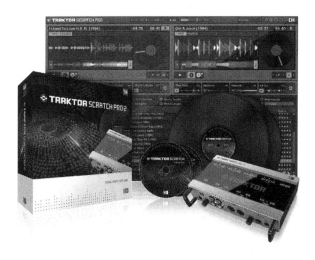

*Traktor Scratch Pro 2, an example of a DVS system
that converts existing DJ set-ups into digital DJ
set-ups able to control DJ software.*

DVS systems also require a laptop and DJ software, but this time they ingeniously let the DJ use any existing gear to DJ from. So let's say a DJ already owns a traditional pair of turntables and mixer. By plugging a special DVS device (sometimes called a 'breakout box' or 'DVS audio interface') between the mixer and the record decks, and plugging a lead from the same device into a laptop running the DJ program, the DJ can then use special 'control vinyl' or 'timecode vinyl' (records that, instead of containing music, contain computer code) to control the DJ software.

It's important to note here that despite the 'V' of DVS standing for vinyl, actually all DVS systems come with control/timecode CDs too. As most DJ booths in the 21st century contain at least a pair of DJ CD decks (and hardly any contain turntables any more), this means that, armed with a pair of these special CDs, a laptop and a DVS box, a DVS DJ can play just about anywhere. One beauty of DVS systems is they don't rely on the equipment in the venue being particularly modern or digital-friendly; as long as the CD players can play CDs and the mixer can mix, a DVS set-up will allow the modern DJ to play. Venue owners tend to be much more accepting of DVS than controllers for some reason too.

If you want a DVS system at home, then you'll have to invest in the 'original' gear to tack it on to as well, so this kind of set-up usually appeals to people who already own DJ gear and are trying to drag it into the modern age.

Modular Midi DJ systems

*The Akai Pro AFX, an example of a modular DJ controller
that can be added to a DJ system to do a specific task.
This way, DJs can mix and match to build a system
that achieves their desired specification.*

It is possible to mix and match specialised DJ or Midi controllers to create custom DJ systems, in the same way audiophiles assemble hi-fi systems from separates. For instance, you can buy the mixer section of a DJ controller, a couple of specialised deck controllers, and other types of button boxes, and plug them all into the laptop running your DJ software to create a control surface that recreates whatever's on your mind. There's a whole subculture around such boxes and gadgets and the mapping thereof ('mapping' refers to programming your DJ software so the controls on your controllers do whatever you wish).

From a more practical standpoint than bedroom tinkering, though, modular controllers can be useful if you want to add a few extra controls to a DVS set-up, or don't want to hulk an all-in-one DJ controller around with you everywhere. You can distil your DJing style into something you can perform on one or two small devices that, for instance, could fit more easily into cramped DJ booths.

The most important thing to remember when choosing parts for a modular DJ set-up is that, unless you're adding to a DVS system, you'll need one of those modular parts to contain an audio interface or you'll need to buy one separately. An audio interface is an important part of any digital DJ set-up, because without it, you'll not have the outputs you need for your headphones and speakers. You may also need a powered USB hub to extend the number of USB sockets on your computer in order to plug everything in.

Pro DJ gear

A Pioneer DJ pro system of the type that is installed in the best clubs worldwide.

Watch any festival DJ set or get a peek into the DJ booth of any self-respecting super-club, and the gear the DJ will be using is what we're talking about here. Pro DJ gear is the modern incarnation of the old-fashioned 'two record decks/CD players and a mixer' set-up. A modern DJ set-up of this type typically contains two or more media players and a digital DJ mixer, and is both expensive and highly capable. The most modern set-ups from the likes of Pioneer DJ (easily the industry leader) and others are basically huge modular DJ controllers, having big colour touch screens showing waveform and library information similar to your computer screen, and rivalling DJ controllers in features having played many years of catch up.

While these systems work best with music prepared on USB drives using their respective manufacturers' custom software (in exactly the same way as the subset of DJ controllers that don't need a laptop for performing from do), depending on model and manufacturer they also plug directly in to laptops running their own or other brands of DJ software via a protocol called 'HID' (human interface device). They can be used with DVS timecode software, often without the need for DVS boxes or even CDs, as the capabilities are all built in: the computer plugs directly into the mixer, and if the DJ set-up is all networked together (the best will be), one lead is all it takes to get set up and going.

These systems are fantastic and the learning curve from bedroom to booth will be very short if you invest in one of them, but they take up a lot of room and cost an awful lot of money compared to an equivalent DJ controller that can do similar things function-wise. Hence they're not the best choice for most DJs when they start out.

Legacy DJ gear (old-style turntables/CD players and mixers)

A Technics turntable, the original DJ deck. A pair of these and an analogue audio mixer was the pinnacle of DJ gear right up until the digital revolution began with CD players and then DJ controllers and software.

If you're a new DJ, you may be harbouring some romantic notion of 'going purist'. Or you may already own, or be offered cheap, an old DJ system of this type, and be wondering whether it'll be up to the job.

If you want to DJ with turntables and vinyl because you think that's how DJing should be done, it's a noble sentiment, but think hard before committing. The downsides of this decision are that very little music is available on vinyl as compared to digitally, and you'll find yourself spending much more than digital DJs to acquire this music. Plus, very few venues have turntables any more. For these reasons, I'd never recommend anyone starting out like this – or if you do, add a DVS system so you can DJ digitally as well.

If you're considering investing in basic DJ CD decks (that maybe don't have slots for USB drives, which will tie you to playing CDs), the case isn't so clear cut. One of the joys of modern DJing is that you can assemble a great music collection from digital downloads, but you can still do that with a CD-only system: you can burn your music to CDs yourself then play it in your CD DJ set-up, or you can add on a DVS system. As even very cheap DJ CD players tend to have USB slots nowadays, you could put your music files on to USB drives and DJ using those too.

Compared to DJ controllers and modern pro DJ gear, such systems are severely limited in what you can do with them, and so ultimately less fun to DJ on. But the leap from such a system to the pro DJ booth isn't huge (which is an advantage if you want gear at home that feels similar to DJ booth gear), and systems like this are still popular in large areas of the world, including many smaller clubs and bar-type venues. Such a system at home would make a good practice set-up for the DJ who will be playing out a lot using the club's gear, especially when bought with a DVS system.

How to choose your DJ set-up

So now you know about the types of gear out there, what should you go for? For most DJs, the answer is definitely a modern DJ controller. If you're a new DJ, simply work out what you can spend, find a few DJ controllers around your price range that are designed to work with the software brand you prefer, and buy one that you like the look of. (You're going to be standing in front of it for many hours, hopefully lots of those in public, so it has to be something that doesn't make you feel silly.) Try and get a sense as to whether it's used by other DJs like you, for which comments under online reviews are a good place to do some scouting, such as on my website: www.digitaldjtips.com

If you really don't want to join the vast majority of DJs happily playing from modern DJ controllers both at home and out and about, and instead you want to invest in one of the other types of system, again, find one that works with the software you prefer. You'll find fewer choices (for instance, if you want to DJ in pro DJ booths 'natively', you'll usually find that means buying a system from market leader Pioneer DJ), and you'll find your choices become less straightforward (assembling a modular set-up can be mind-numbing for a beginner because you don't really know enough about your own style of DJing to recognise what options are going to work best for you, plus technically they are harder to set up).

If you are hell-bent on buying a DJ set-up of two basic CD players and a mixer, but can't afford to spend much, seriously consider adding a DVS system to broaden your options. DVS is also a good move if you own DJ gear from years gone by and want to start playing the modern way. And as I said above, commit to vinyl-only DJing at your peril; pretty much the whole of the pro DJing world moved away from this way of DJing for a reason. Despite its undeniable appeal as the purist way of doing things, it has too many disadvantages for today's DJ.

If you're still stuck, review my suggestions at the end of the software chapter about checking what your friends and DJs in your local venues are using, and remember that a small, cheap, simple DJ controller really is all you need to learn the skills in this book. If in doubt, buy such a device now and upgrade later when you know what you're doing; it can always double up as your back-up system when you are ready to go a little more pro.

Your DJ gear really isn't all that important in the long run. Not only will you likely change it more regularly than you might want to acknowledge now, but ultimately, a good DJ sees any DJ set-up as a tool to get the end result.

So go off and get yourself a DJ system. In the next chapter, we're going to look at some of the other stuff you'll need.

Other Items You'll Need

Introduction

As with most hobbies, there are a handful of essential things that may not be immediately obvious to you when you think about your initial gear purchases, and others that are optional but you may be considering buying. Even if you put some of these purchases off until later, it's worth thinking about them now, if only to start the fun process of researching your future world-conquering set-up.

A pair of DJ headphones, in this instance, the Sennheiser HD8 model. Note the moving ear cups, and the closed heavily padded design.

Probably the first thing that needs to be on your gear list is a decent pair of headphones. They are important for DJs because you need to be able to listen clearly to stuff your audience *isn't* hearing, and the usual way to do that is through using headphones.

DJ headphones need to be, in order of importance: isolating (i.e. they are well padded to effectively cut off outside sound), loud, durable, adjustable (not for a comfortable fit, but so you can wear them with one ear cup on and one off your ears), and foldable (for easy transport). Many DJs, myself included, prefer a coiled cable so it doesn't get under your feet when you're standing next to your gear, but at the same time lets you walk away from your gear with the headphones still on. Some models offer detachable cables with an extra style of cable too, so you may get a short straight cable for use with your phone as well as the longer DJ cable. Finally, while over ear models dominate, smaller on ear designs are preferred by some, and the latter definitely work better if you're buying one set for both DJing and when you're out and about. Go for closed back rather than open back designs.

For just learning, frankly any kind of headphones that have a headband will do (sorry, your phone earbuds are definitely out), so it's worth digging around at home to see if you have some. That said, you can get workable DJ models for as little as £20, although of course you can easily go up to many times that.

Speakers/PA system

A range of modern DJ monitor speakers, designed for home or studio use. These are from one of the leading brands, KRK.

Already got a TV sound bar, or a hi-fi, or even just a loud portable speaker? As long as your existing speaker set-up sounds good and goes loud enough for you to be able to truly fill the room with music, it will probably do fine for DJ practice. All that's necessary is to be able to set it up near to your DJ system (see next chapter), and for it to have a socket so you can plug in your DJ controller using a cable (i.e. not Bluetooth, AirPlay, or any other wireless system).

If you want to invest in something better or something specially for DJing with, then you have two choices: studio monitor-style speakers or a small PA system. Studio monitors are dedicated speakers meant for DJ/producer types. They are usually sold individually (i.e. you buy two), and each has its own amplifier or amplifiers built in as well as its own power supply and music inputs. As they're separate, you run the left-hand output of your DJ system to the left-hand speaker, and the right-hand output to the right speaker. In price, good ones range from around £200 per speaker upwards.

Such speakers are great if you want the very best sound quality and you never (and I repeat, *never*) want to use them in a party situation. Studio monitors can and probably will end up broken if you use them at parties as they're not physically or electrically designed for the kind of stress you'll put them under in a party situation. If you want to buy a speaker system that you can use at parties, a small PA system is better. Many such systems have the beauty of being small enough to use for practising at home, too, so you only need buy one system. Get one with tripods for your speakers and long cables, and you'll have all you need for both practice and parties.

If you can afford it, buying a subwoofer as well (a big floor-standing speaker designed only to pump out bass) will make your system sound better when you're in a full room of people; you can always leave this in your car boot or garage rather than humping it up the stairs to your bedroom studio as your PA will work fine without it for home use.

Miscellaneous things

If you're planning on DJing from USB drives rather than a laptop, obviously you're going to need a USB stick or two to keep your music on. Buy a durable design with the biggest capacity you can afford.

A moulded cover to protect the delicate controls of your DJ gear is a good idea. This is one of a range from a company called Decksaver.

Protecting your gear is a smart move. A decent case, back pack, or trolley will help keep your controller or other gear looking new, and you could invest in a dustcover too (an old towel thrown over your gear will do the job, but moulded made-to-fit acrylic covers are available, and are a better choice). Raising your laptop higher than your DJ controller using a laptop stand will help you to see the screen properly (go for something easily foldable and sturdy). Make yourself heard with a microphone (wired are cheapest, make sure your choice will plug in to whatever microphone socket is available to you on your DJ gear, and go for a dynamic mic).

Finally, make sure you figure out the leads you need and get them all, plus spares - and don't forget a decent power extension cable, heavy duty and with a high amp fuse if you're going to be running a PA system through it too.

Setting Everything Up

Introduction

If you're serious about learning to DJ, you're going to be spending a lot of time behind the decks, whether those decks are a simple iPad app or the exact same sprawling set-up sported by your local super-club. Setting your equipment up properly in a workspace that's conducive to creativity (and kind on your back) is therefore an essential first step. Likewise, having a reliable back-up routine in place for your music and DJ program data is also something you ought to set up right at the start. 'Set and forget' goes the saying, so let's cover these things right now before we move on to the second section of this book, which is all about the music.

Setting up your home DJ workspace

Not everyone has a studio space or room they can dedicate to their DJing, far away from distractions and moaning neighbours. Whichever nook and cranny of your home you decide to set up your practice area in, and whatever gear you have, a few ground rules will help you to make a success of it:

Make sure your table is at the right height. Nothing spells 'back pain' quicker than DJing standing at a table you're meant to be sitting at. Most DJs prefer to practise standing up, so make sure your gear is at about the height of a standard kitchen work surface. If all you have is a sitting-height table, try perching your DJ controller on the box it came in as a temporary measure, or use a beer crate or similar to raise it up.

Have the speakers as close to you as possible. Speaker positioning is crucial for DJing. Speakers that are to your left and right, at head height (or angled up at your head if they're on the same surface as your DJ gear), and no more than two or three feet from you will sound better, and make it easier when it comes to learning skills like manual beatmixing. Believe it or not, your brain starts to notice the small delay it takes the sound to reach you when speakers are only, say, ten feet or so from your head, and that makes DJing harder and so less fun. Plus, the closer the speakers are to you, the quieter you can have them for sufficient DJing volume.

Try not to face the wall. This one isn't always possible, but you'll gain from facing out into a room. Not only is this going to make it easier to have impromptu house parties, but it'll help you visualise playing to a real audience, which in turn will help you to think right from the off about body language and how you'll perform when you do get out in public - skills you can't start to learn too early.

Make it somewhere you only go to DJ. Not necessarily a room on its own, but a corner that is reserved for your DJ practice sessions. It's good for motivation to dedicate a space, however small, to your hobby. If you can leave your gear set up there, all the better, because it'll make it easier to get going when it comes to practice time.

Getting your laptop and hardware working smoothly

As long as you did the due diligence on your laptop outlined earlier, you shouldn't encounter problems with getting it all working OK. Follow the instructions that came with your DJ hardware with regards to software downloading and installation, and if the audio isn't doing what you expect it to (the most common issue), look under 'Audio Configuration' or 'Audio Settings' in the manual to find the necessary tweaks.

While DJ software isn't hugely demanding on the resources of your computer, this is a performance game, and so any glitches or hiccoughs are potentially going to be more annoying than if your computer were just being used as an office PC. So it does pay to follow a few steps to make mishaps less likely.

(I remember forgetting to silence unnecessary system sounds on a Windows PC I was DJing from in a nightclub once, and when I turned it off, the Windows closing down motif blasted over a 10K sound system to a couple of hundred startled late-night clubbers. Cue sheepish blushing from the DJ booth...)

So when you're preparing your computer for DJing, consider making the following adjustments:

Switch off any internet, network, and wireless connectivity. While there is sometimes a case for having internet on (some DJ software can stream from music online as you play nowadays), having your computer connected to Bluetooth, Wi-Fi, Ethernet, or any other unnecessary networks is asking for trouble.

Disable auto-updating of software. You *do not* want your computer announcing to you that it has downloaded some critical updates and is going to reboot in fifteen minutes. That's an alert box to breathe fear into the heart of any performing DJ…

Close down all programs you're not using. Programs running in the background that you don't want or need are usually fine when surfing or working at your PC, but not so fine when you're DJing from it. They take system resources and can cause performance issues, which can lead to glitches in the audio or more sluggish overall performance (songs loading slowly and so on). Best to pare right down to your DJ software.

Turn off all notifications, banners, popups, and windows. Again, common sense really, but you don't want these popping up and sounding off as you practise DJing. While you're at it, why not go to your sound settings and turn off all unnecessary system sounds? It'd avoid embarrassing situations like my story above…

What to do if your laptop gives you problems

By far the most common issue when DJing using laptops is the DJ software momentarily finding it doesn't have enough system resources to do its thing (this is such an important variable that many programs actually have a 'CPU load' or similar indicator so you can keep an eye on it). This usually shows itself through glitchy or momentarily freezing graphics and crackly sound or, again, momentary dropouts in audio.

While alarming, the graphic freezing usually rights itself, but can sometimes be fixed by looking for settings that let you alter the graphics performance of your software (look for 'refresh rate' settings). Audio is obviously much bigger an issue, and the culprit here is usually the 'latency' or 'audio buffer' setting being too low. This governs the length of time between you doing something (starting a tune, stopping it, and so on) and that action coming out of the audio interface to head off to the speakers. Too high, and there's a perceptible delay. Too low, and the computer can't cope. Find the setting, and adjust it so it is as low as possible without any glitches when you do your stuff. Many DJs then like to increase that setting by one notch to err a little on the safe side.

Getting your back-up routine into place

Stories abounded in DJ circles back in the vinyl days about Great Lost Record Tragedies. We used to have to put our record cases into the hold luggage when flying to gigs, never knowing if we'd see them again. Sometimes, when girlfriends fell out with DJ boyfriends and kicked them out (here's a DJ joke for you: what do you call a DJ without a girlfriend? Homeless), their collections would follow, sometimes from a first floor window. In all of these circumstances, DJs spoke of a vacuous feeling like nothing else.

The moral for modern DJs is really simple: back up your hard drive. Your music is the tool of your trade, and in this book you're going to learn how to grow your music collection so it's an extension of how you think and feel – don't ever let there be any chance of you losing that collection. Before moving on to the next step, when we're going to start gathering the music that'll make you the DJ you are going to be, I'd recommend you nail this one.

It honestly doesn't matter how you do it. Your choices are things like a network storage device in your home, a detachable hard drive you keep in the top of a wardrobe, a cloud service such as Dropbox, or just a big USB drive you copy everything over to. The golden rules are do it regularly (I suggest weekly) and put it in your calendar so you don't ever forget, and always back up to two separate places that aren't physically the same – so if you back up to a spare hard drive at home, keep a USB copy at work, or have a second copy in the cloud. Whatever works for you. Just do it.

By the way, if you choose not to back up your whole computer (and if you're backing up to USB pen drive, you won't be able to as its capacity isn't big enough) and instead just want to back up your music, at the very minimum make sure you back up the folder or folders you keep your music files in as well as the folder your DJ software keeps its information in. Check your DJ software documentation for details of where the latter folder will be. It is where important DJ performance data is kept about your music files, and while losing it wouldn't be as catastrophic as losing the files themselves, it could potentially make an awful lot of work for you once your collection grows a bit and you start to customise the data you hold on your songs.

OK, so with our foundations all laid and our system built, it's time to move on to the reason you probably got into this whole thing in the first place: the music. That's what the whole of the next step is about.

Step Two: Music

In this step, you'll learn everything you need to know about finding, choosing, buying, organising, and preparing the most important thing for any DJ: your music. You'll meet the Playlist Pyramid, a tool I use to teach this process, we'll cover methods for hearing more music than everyone else, and ways of capturing song titles and artists so it all becomes second nature. I'll give you a solid framework for how to make a shortlist of music you may want to buy, and talk you through the mechanics of actually getting it into your digital collection. I'll help you to make sense of all those music files by properly organising and tagging them, and show you how to use artwork to bring them to life in your software. We'll discuss using music library software, and finally getting your carefully chosen tunes into your DJ program and ready to DJ with.

How To Discover Great Music

Introduction

Part of your job as a DJ is to hear more of the world's music than your average person, so you can pick the best of that music for your own collection - music that talks to you personally. Armed with a collection of tunes you really care about and the DJing formula taught in this book, you'll be ready to play DJ sets that please both your crowds and you.

It all starts with music discovery. Music discovery is the first stage of a process I illustrate with the Playlist Pyramid.

THE PLAYLIST PYRAMID

Right there at the base of the pyramid we have all the music that's ever been recorded in the whole world.

The Playlist Pyramid allows you to visualise the process you'll go through as a DJ to filter the music that's out there, from everything that exists to the exact handful of tunes you end up playing in any given DJ set. We'll work with it a lot more in this step of this process, but for now, note that the bottom of the pyramid is where you'll find all the music that's ever been recorded in the whole world.

Now, if you're hearing *less* music than everyone else, or just buying the stuff you hear other DJs play, then how can you possibly make a good job of standing out from the next DJ? So we need to build the pure simplicity of listening to lots and lots of music into your life.

Here are the five golden rules.

Five rules of music discovery

Listen to music anywhere and everywhere. Your job is to build music into your life to such an extent that it's harder to avoid it than it is to keep listening. Got a buzzer-style alarm clock? Get a clock radio instead, and tune in to a music station as you wake up. Make sure you have speakers in every room of your house (Bluetooth, Sonos, whatever). Keep your iPad, iPhone or MP3 player packed with music for when you're out and about. Set every preset on your car radio to a different music channel. If you're allowed headphones at work, wear 'em. When you go out, try to go to a music bar rather than a sports bar (for instance). Subscribe to a streaming music service such as Apple Music or Spotify, and make sure you get your money's worth. Wear headphones at the gym, walking the dog, while running, on planes...you get the idea. No silence.

Listen to anything and everything. This isn't about being painfully cool, it's about listening to music - any music. From death metal to kiddies' TV themes, classical to country, this is your chance to hear music of all types, not just music you'd play, buy or even particularly like. The point is to have music on. Indeed, it is often better to listen to stuff that makes you uncomfortable - that's when you broaden your tastes and become more knowledgeable.

Don't think too much about it. This is at first a hard one to do, but you will get better at it. Listening to music 24/7 is not about having long debates with yourself over whether what you're hearing is cool or not, whether you could play it in a DJ set, or anything else cerebral, for that matter. If you cave in to consciously grading, sorting and organising the music you hear, you'll be exhausted pretty quickly and find yourself turning it off to get a break from yourself. This is about feelings, not thoughts; emotions, not reasons. When a joke makes you laugh, do you analyse why it made you laugh? Of course not. Nor should you analyse the music you've got on.

Notice what interests you. As from now you'll be playing music all the time, and as you're not going to over analyse it, you're inevitably going to switch off and almost forget you have music on at all. That's exactly what we want, because now you'll be listening like a 'normal' person, not a DJ. And when something grabs your attention, it will do so not via the critical faculties of a hard-to-please DJ, but because deep down you like something about whatever the piece of music is. It's important to realise that *what* it is you like about that tune is not important. You may notice it because it's a great song, because it really annoys you, because it sounds like something else in your collection, because it's the first tune you've heard loud for ages – whatever. Learn to acknowledge that something has got your attention, take note of the fact, and get on with your day.

Religiously note all such tunes. Using a note-taking app on your smartphone, or Shazam (the music recognition app for iOS and Android, which is great if you don't know the title of a particular piece of music), or just good old pen and paper, scribble down names, artists, even snippets of lyrics for you to Google later if that's all you can get. Just try and get some kind of placeholder for that tune in your system.

Four ideas to get you started

In order to achieve the above every day of your life from now on, it's true that you're going to need a bit of planning and preparation. Spend a couple of hours doing some or all of the following things so you've always got something to listen to. You can revisit this exercise weekly as part of your choosing and shortlisting music session (more about that in the next chapter), because there are always new services, shows and technologies, and it pays to shake things up sometimes.

Get loads of music on your iPad, iPhone, or smartphone. As mentioned above, you really do need to subscribe to a streaming service, such as Apple Music or Spotify. These services let you keep music offline to play when you don't have an internet connection, so make the most of that fact and pack your device with albums by artists you think you may like, compilations, playlists curated by the service's staff - whatever. This is your fallback for all times, so make sure it's full of new music.

Find out when the chart show is broadcast in your area, and tune in religiously. Doesn't matter whether you want to be the most underground DJ on the block or play chart music yourself - your local chart show tells you what people near you are buying, streaming and downloading. There is always value to be had by keeping up to date with this information, if only to find that the underground track you thought was your little discovery is actually in the Top 10.

Choose a music web/iOS/Android app or two, and learn how they work. There are apps out there that trawl the music blogs, bringing you aggregated 'hot tracks' from across the web. There are apps where people upload their own productions, radio shows, and DJ mixes. There are services that bring web feeds from local broadcast radio stations worldwide to anyone, anywhere. There are even sites that broadcast other DJs' sets live. Find one or two you like, and use them.

Look at names like Hype Machine, SoundCloud and Mixcloud.

Don't forget about the music you already like or own. You may have been collecting music for decades, or you may have very little, but you certainly have artists you like, and songs you love. Listen to all of this stuff too, and make a note of the tracks that particularly stand out for you in the same way as if it were new music to you.

THE PLAYLIST PYRAMID

This chapter has taught you to move to the second tier of the Playlist Pyramid, where you've heard a wide variety of the music that's out there, and naturally made a note of a whole bunch of stuff you may or may not decide later to go to the next tier with.

Keeping an open mind

This is music discovery, not critical appraisal. This is the one time when you really do put quantity over quality - listen to anything! If you're going to become a tastemaker, someone who spots new trends, you're going to have to have your ears open, and not only to the stuff you think you're going to want to use in your DJ sets. As you'll see in the next chapter, there's plenty of time for formally thinking through the music you've identified as being interesting in your day-to-day discovery sessions.

How To Choose And Buy Music

Introduction

Back in the days of record stores and scarcity, here's how my Saturdays used to go: 8am, take the number 86 bus into town, head down to the 'record shop street' and hit the stores, just as the distributors' vans arrived with this week's 12-inch vinyl delivery. It was always a scramble for attention as the shops were busy with dozens of other DJs doing the same, and equally, it was hard to get a listening post in order to audition the piles of vinyl I'd selected, but that didn't stop me. (When my career took off, I was one of the privileged few who were allowed to use the private basement in my favourite store - Eastern Bloc Records, Manchester, England - where I could take as long as I wanted listening to my tunes, on real speakers instead of battered old headphones, but that privilege took years to earn.)

Many DJs go glassy eyed remembering record shop culture, but they forget the queueing for listening posts, broken headphones, and guesswork involved in picking the right tunes on the spot. The truth is that if you do it right, your tune shortlisting and purchasing in the digital age can be every bit as rewarding and fruitful as those record shop trips of a whole generation's halcyon days - and this chapter is all about showing you how.

Before we get going, the first rule is to do this regularly. While much of what you've been asked to do has been either one-off (buy some gear, get yourself set up) or background stuff (have some music on and note down the stuff that interests you), this is a timetabled piece of work. I suggest you do it weekly, and put it in your calendar at the same time each week so it becomes habit.

The second rule is to follow the system below exactly. Shortlisting and buying music can easily turn into a whole day of listening to more and more tunes, disappearing down obscure musical rabbit holes as the whim takes us. Back in the record store days we couldn't do this (there was a queue for the listening posts to start with), so we had to focus on efficiently processing what was in front of us. That's what this procedure is designed to achieve for you in your digital shortlisting.

Shortlisting music

THE PLAYLIST PYRAMID

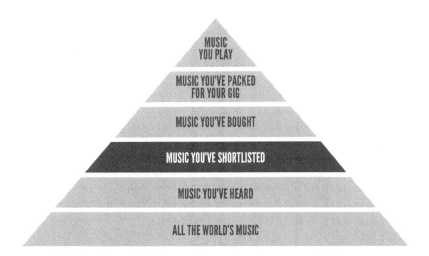

Shortlisting your music is the third tier of the Playlist Pyramid, and a crucial step between stuff you've simply made a note of and the point where you actually choose to buy it.

So, Saturday morning, or whenever you choose, here's your routine. To start with, assemble all your notes: Shazamed tracks, scribbled stuff from your diary, stuff you've added to a shortlist playlist in your streaming service, track names from your mobile phone's note-taking function, whatever. Get them all in one place, and take some time to research songs that you want but can't remember or never found out the names of. (Hint: Googling unusual phrases in lyrics often uncovers track names for you.) This was what we used to do back in the day on paper before leaving the house. You need that definitive hit list for the week.

Next, try to find and listen to every piece of music you've noted, all the way through if you can. Use decent headphones or have it nice and loud, and hear high quality versions if you can. Most online stores only let you hear a minute or so of a tune, which isn't really enough, so look for the tunes on your streaming service or YouTube - anywhere you can hear them all the way through. (In the record shop, this was where we'd head to the listening post with our pile.)

As you're doing this, put anything you decide you still like and would enjoy hearing again, whether definitely for your DJing or just because it interests you, in one 'pile', and strike off the rest. If you're not sure about a tune, dump it. Keep going until you're done with your noted tunes. What's left is your week's shortlist. (Back in the record store, this would be our 'listen again' pile, as we knew we couldn't afford all of them. Hard decisions lay ahead.)

Often, this exercise will throw up tunes you hadn't heard until today. A track you dialled up may have been on a great-looking compilation album, so you dug around it and found a few more good songs. An artist whose record piqued your interest may have a ton of other releases, and you had a listen and loved a few. You may have discovered a label you hadn't heard of and taken the time to check out some of their stuff only to hit a goldmine. That's cool, add those tunes to your shortlist too. Just remember that rabbit hole…

Now, the most important part. You will avoid a lot of wasted time and money by asking the following big questions about *each and every tune you have on your shortlist*. These questions are designed to force you to be crystal clear about your reasons for liking the tunes. Be strict about this; remember, your job as a DJ is to filter the world's music into perfectly formed sets, right for every occasion – and you won't do that without making some hard choices along the way.

For each tune, ask yourself:

Is it danceable? Usually, of course, the answer to this needs to be a resounding yes. You may love a tune for home listening, but if it isn't going to work on the dancefloor, you really don't want it in your DJ collection. The exception to this rule would be 'DJ tools' – things you use in your set for effect or a specific purpose. Think classical music for a dramatic intro, or an *a cappella* that you know you'd like to weave in somewhere, or a famous movie theme you want to surprise people with.

Can I see myself playing this tune in a DJ set? If you are a huge fan of Latin music but know you're never going to get any gigs playing that genre, not much point buying it for your DJ sets. If you're planning on being a mobile DJ, collecting obscure German techno isn't likely to roll with your crowds. You have to ask whether there's any chance of you using each track in any DJ set, actual or imagined, in the near future. If not, add it to a playlist on your streaming service for non-DJ day-to-day listening and move on.

Does this tune complement what I already own? This is a more subtle question, but as your collection grows, it's an increasingly important one. Ever heard the expression 'capsule wardrobe'? A capsule wardrobe describes a set of clothing items that can be worn together in any number of combinations and still look good. By owning relatively few items of clothing that have been carefully purchased, a person can sport a huge number of great looks. Approach your music collection in exactly the same way. You're looking for a selection of tunes that form a coherent, flexible whole, which means tunes that stand up on their merits, but contrast well with each other: a nice mix of vocals, instrumentals, slow tunes, quick tunes, old stuff, new stuff, familiar songs, obscure gems, and so on. Another way of framing this question is 'Am I buying too much of the same thing?', because if you are, you'll end up not playing much of it. Look for the *best* examples of as many types of music that you like as you can find.

Is this tune good enough to replace something else in my collection? This is the final test, and it's a hard one. When you're just starting out, it can be tempting not to ask it, because, well, your collection isn't so large. But ask it, nonetheless. Later, when your collection is 500, 1,000 or 2,500 tunes, you're going to hit the point where you've got too much stuff to keep front of mind meaningfully. And at that point, the best policy is definitely one in, one out.

So what's going to leave your collection in order for this new tune you're considering to enter? Asking this question will force you to decide if *you only like it because it reminds you of something you already own*. If you decide that's true, but actually it builds on and betters that tune, then fine, get the new one - but remove the other tune. Remember, if two tunes don't complement each other (because they're basically doing the same thing), you only have room for one of them.

Buying music

So, any tune that passes all these questions, add to a 'to buy' list. Back in the record store, this is where we'd have, say, the ten tunes we could actually afford (whittled down from thirty after some painful decision making) and be heading to the counter. You're going to do the same: go to your online music store of choice and add the tunes to your cart. It's usual to have to trawl a few stores to get them all, but Googling 'buy (name of tune)' will usually find you a source. Now buy them, and any you can't buy right now, leave on your list for when they become available.

What format to buy music in

The vast majority of the world's DJs buy music in 320kbps MP3 format, which is a compressed file format, giving them relatively small (in size) music files that sound virtually indistinguishable from the originals. It is the preferred format in most DJ stores (the notable exception being Apple's iTunes store, which sells its own equivalent,

256kbps AAC format), and also the format used by digital download pools (specialist sites for working DJs that provide DJ music for a monthly subscription, straight from the labels). MP3s tend to be a bit cheaper than WAV files (the uncompressed alternative), are more widely available, and are easier to manage once you have them in your collection because you can embed useful information such as artwork, title, BPM, and even your own comments in the file itself.

Some DJs swear by WAV files or other uncompressed formats because they say they can hear the difference. I can't, but if you're not convinced, do the test yourself and compare the same song bought from the same store in both formats.

Whatever format you buy your music in, there's work to be done on it once it arrives on your hard drive. We'll look at exactly what in the next chapter.

Preparing, Importing And Tagging Your Music

Introduction

THE PLAYLIST PYRAMID

*The remaining chapters in this section concern the fourth
tier of the Playlist Pyramid - the music we've bought
and how to prepare, import, tag and organise it.*

If one mistake rookie DJs make when getting started with regards to music is the 'more is more' error ('real DJs have tens of thousands of tunes, so I'll just download everything I can think of by everyone I can think of...'), a second is coming up with convoluted ways of processing and organising their music collections. 'If I organise my collection better than anyone else,' goes the thinking, 'I'll be able to find tracks quicker, which will make me a better DJ.' With the abundance of clever tools out there in the digital age for cataloguing, filtering and playlisting our digital music collections, it's easy to understand why involved processes for organising our music can sometimes get the better of us.

There are two issues with this way of thinking. Firstly, the more complicated your music processing system, the more likely you are to abandon it and end up with a music collection in a worse mess than if you'd done nothing. And secondly, there is really no need to do any more than the simple universal things I share with you in this chapter in order to organise any digital music collection effectively, whatever the size. Keep it simple and you'll stick with your system for life, it'll serve you well and, best of all, it'll become second nature to you.

I'll divide my simple system for adding music to your collection into three parts: 'Preparing', 'Importing' and 'Tagging'.

Preparing

So you've bought a handful of tunes, maybe imported a few from CDs or even ripped a few from old vinyl. They're all sitting there in your laptop's downloads folder, ready to move across into your DJ collection. There's actually only a single thing I'd recommend before you do that, and that is change each new tune's filename so it follows a standard system. The system I prefer is simply Artist - Title (Remix

Title), for instance: Robin S - Show Me Love (Stonebridge Club Mix).

By doing this, you'll remove extraneous info that often gets included in filenames, the most common being track number. (Remember, we are not interested in whole albums as DJs, so track number isn't necessary.) Even if you throw all of your songs into one single folder at any time, or put them in one pile on a USB stick, by sorting them alphabetically you'll have a workable collection, ordered by artist. In the absence of any other way of slicing and dicing your music (for instance, if you're playing the songs on a very old CD player or sorting them on a strange computer using the file browser), at least that will be available to you.

Importing

As it's pretty much impossible to do more than alter a tune's filename in a Windows Explorer or Mac Finder window, it's time now to add your new tunes to your music library proper. This is where we'll ensure we have all the other information we need for each track, information which is stored inside the music file itself using something called 'ID3 tagging' - namely things like the correct artist, title, artwork (if wanted), genre, and more, and potentially do some organising too.

The first thing you need to do, then, is move those new tunes from your temporary downloads folder or wherever they happen to be to where you keep your collection proper, which is where you'll work on them further. (Always keep your music library in one place on your computer, because this makes it much easier to back it up regularly.)

Should you use iTunes?

Most DJs use iTunes to store, tag and organise their music. You can set it up to add new music to its own Music folder automatically, meaning you can then safely remove new tracks from anywhere else on your computer.

It's not a perfect piece of software for DJs, but nonetheless they use it because they always have (it was the original digital music library, of course). It is a familiar way of handling a digital music collection, it has powerful playlist features, and it makes it easy to put music from iTunes on to an iPod, iPhone or iPad for listening to elsewhere. It is also unique in that its collection is visible within all DJ software, so all your iTunes playlists will be available to you to play from in any DJ software without any extra work on your part, even if you switch software platforms at some point.

If you're going to use iTunes, due to its increasing complexity and the amalgamation of the Apple Music streaming service within it, we recommend you use it only for your DJ music, keeping family videos, podcasts, and non-DJ music away from it, and turning off iTunes Match, iCloud or similar features. If you do want to use it for all these things too, be clear about how you're going to keep your DJ music separate from all that other stuff.

If you don't want to use iTunes, that's fine. Take the principles here and apply them to your choice of workflow. You'll probably want a good ID3 tag editor to let you tweak the artist, title, artwork, and so on, and as far as organising the music goes, you can do so in any DJ software directly, although none has the power of iTunes for this. The important thing, though, is to absorb these principles and find something that works for you.

Tagging

Tagging your DJ music properly is important because it'll let you find stuff quickly. Really, there is only a small amount of information you need about your tunes to do a good job of this for DJing. In iTunes, your chosen ID3 tag editor, or your DJ software itself (whatever you've chosen to use for this), find a music playlist view that shows you all your music listed as rows, and set the software to show all the columns listed below for easy editing.

These are the basic things you ought to be sure you have for each tune:

- Artist
- Title (including any remix or version name)
- Year
- Genre
- BPM.

You may also want to include:

- Album art
- Energy level

Let's look at the above one by one. Artist is easy, although you may have more than one artist (usually it'll be a 'featuring', for instance 'Primary Artist feat. Featured Artist'), and you'll have to decide what to do about artists whose name begins 'The'. Do you drop the 'The' so you don't have loads of artist names clogging up the 'T' section of your library? I keep the 'The', for what it's worth.

When it comes to the track title, this is the right place to keep the remix or version title, and it can be good to put this in separate brackets, or even square brackets, so as not to confuse the remix or version title with any part of the song title that's in brackets itself. As an example: Single Ladies (Put A Ring On It) [Dave Aude Club Mix].

Year is self-explanatory, although it is worth remembering that the track may have been released before you bought it, and often the year will be wrong on downloaded music as it may refer to the year the album the track came from was released, not the year the track itself was released. This can trip you up on tracks from 'Best of' compilations or digitally remastered versions of songs, so make sure you check the release year.

Genre is the category a lot of people mess up on, which is a shame as it's one of the most powerful things to get right.

The bottom line is you need to choose genres that mean something to *you*, and that will help *your* DJing. Let me give you a couple of examples.

Jeff is a mobile DJ who plays for all ages at a variety of gigs. He plays music he divides into the following genres: Pop, Dance, Hip hop, Rock, Disco, Ballads, Country. Sarah, however, is a dance DJ/producer type. She divides her collection into Deep house, Big room house, Electro house, Tech house, Minimal house, and Trance. Jeff could put every single track in Sarah's collection into just one of his categories: 'Dance'.

So who's right? The answer is both of them are. You see, Sarah often plays a whole set of one or two of those types of music (maybe a minimal house build-up, followed by some big room house). If she didn't divide her collection up into a handful of genres meaningful to her, it would rob her of the ability to sort her collection quickly depending on the type of music she wanted to play.

Jeff, on the other hand, plays a wider selection of music and his genres are broader, yet for him they make perfect sense (he rotates a bit of hip hop with pop and dance at a typical mobile gig, ending with some country, rock and ballads). For Jeff, subdividing these genres makes no sense. Furthermore, he may be a bit loose with his definitions, for instance throwing funk in with disco and R&B in with hip hop, and again he'd be right, because Jeff is organising tunes into piles that serve a purpose *for him*.

However (and this is crucial), for both Jeff and Sarah, the genres their tunes are labelled with when they *arrive* mean nothing. Absolutely be ready to throw the labelled genres when you buy a tune right out of the window. Just because a tune is labelled 'Deep house' when you buy it does not mean you have to keep it that way. If to you it is pop, change it to that label. The important thing is that when you dial up all the tunes you've labelled as one genre or another, they feel coherent to you, and you could imagine them on a mixtape or in a set together. Learn to be irreverent with your musical genres. You can always change them again later.

This is the only caveat once you start relabelling your tunes' genres: don't fall into the trap of using the 'Genre' column to label non-musical qualities of tunes, 'Girl-friendly' or 'End of night favourite' or 'Warm-up tune', for instance. This information best belongs in the catch-all 'Comments' tag. Keep genre for musical descriptions.

So moving on, BPM means beats per minute and refers to the speed or tempo of the tune. When you first add a tune to your collection, it may or may not already appear in the BPM column, depending on whether the store you bought it from included that information. Don't worry about this for now: your DJ software will automatically add this for you later on.

Album art (or Release art) is well worth adding, especially if you're a visual type of person or have ever owned a physical record or CD collection. If the tunes were once in a physical collection of yours, head off to Google Images or similar to find the cover you recognise. If not, again, Google Images can find you a nice cool-looking release cover for most tunes (especially helpful if you bought a single track from a cheesy compilation album and want something a bit cooler as the album art).

Finally, Energy level. This is a bona fide secret weapon which can be especially powerful when used alongside your Genre column. Quite simply, when you listen to a track, how much does it make you want to dance? In other words, how energetic is it? Does it bang along, all big drops and overblown synth lines, or is it more subtle? Giving your tracks a subjective rating of say one to five on an energy level scale (have a guess, you can always fine tune later) can help you plan a set that rises gently and avoid accidentally playing something too full-on too early in your set.

Now, there is actually no 'Energy level' column in iTunes. You could put a number in the Comment column, or (as I do) use iTunes's 'Rating star' column. As you're being particular about every single tune you allow into your DJ collection, logically your rating for them *all* is five, making this a redundant column, so why not use it for energy rating instead? The only issue is that DJ software often doesn't show this column, but it is possible to set up Smart Playlists in iTunes that automatically include all tracks with each of the five energy ratings, and these do show in DJ software.

By the way, a great resource for checking a lot of the above information online is a site called Discogs (http://www.discogs.com), where record collectors have meticulously organised decades' worth of music releases. If you're missing a year, or a remix title, or some cover art, this is the place to do your research.

Now you've properly tagged everything, we can move on to organising your music.

Organising Your Music

Introduction

I can still recall my beloved DJ room back at the height of the vinyl days. I'd built heavy duty shelving across one wall to house my thousands of records, and I had a designer steel console for my turntables and mixer. On the floor were several record boxes and bags, some of which had DJ sets I'd played recently still in them, and propped up around the feet of the DJ console were piles of records not yet shelved or bagged - newly arrived promotional mailings, stuff I'd bought but not played or sorted yet, twenty tunes for a mixtape I was working on, a mini disco set I'd been experimenting with a couple of nights back, and so on. It was a beautiful thing, creative chaos, yet I knew where everything was and where it all belonged.

The big problem with digital music is that we need tools to help us reach this kind of visceral meaningful chaos - this type of hands-on intimacy - with what are essentially zeros and ones stored on a computer hard drive. We are already in a good place with this thanks to having been careful with the music we've bought for our DJing in the first place, and making sure we've added the right information about it and brought it into some kind of music library that we are comfortable about using. Now we need to finish the process by getting comfortable with how we organise that music, slice 'n' dice it, playlist it - or, to go back to my DJ room, how we get to having those little propped-up piles of special tunes knocking around that reflect work we have to do with our tracks or thoughts we're having about mixtapes, forthcoming DJ sets, whatever. That's what this chapter is about.

Why this is important

Organising your complete collection a little bit further once you've got it all in one place is something that, once you're in the habit of doing it, will become an essential part of the way you think about music; an extension of the little connections you're making between your tracks in your mind. It can be helpful in so many ways, for instance:

It helps you to get to know your music better. Any work you do inside your DJ music library has the added benefit of helping you to learn more about those songs, and knowing your songs better leads to better DJ sets. Hint: never do any work in your DJ collection if something isn't actually playing. If you find yourself organising your music in silence, hit 'Play' on anything at all before you continue.

It gives you playlists to listen to away from your computer. As you further slice 'n' dice your music, you naturally come up with shorter sequences that have something in common. These are shoe-ins for uploading to your iPod or smartphone to give you something exciting to listen to all those times you're not actually sitting down doing 'DJ stuff'.

It helps you to pack great DJ sets. Later on I'll explain to you how to 'pack' a DJ set formally before each and every gig (and why this is so important), but for now, know that getting into the habit of further organising your main collection not only helps you learn the tools for packing DJ sets when the time comes, but will give you lots of ideas for those sets too. Effectively, you're doing some of the work ahead of time.

How to do it

The quickest way to organise your music further is to sort your master collection by one of its parameters inside iTunes or whatever music library program you're using. (This might be your DJ software itself if you're bypassing using anything else for this stage.) You usually do this by clicking on the column heading of the parameter you're interested in to order by that field. So if you want to order by genre, click on the 'Genre' column to order by A to Z (and click again to toggle to Z to A), and you can now scroll down through your genres - all the house in one part of the list, all the hip hop in another, all the pop in another, and so on. Of course, you can do so by year, BPM, artist, and so on. Often this is all you'll need to get to a pile of tunes you want quickly (for instance, clicking 'date added' will get all your latest tunes to the top of the pile).

But the fantastic thing about digital music collections is that you can organise your main collection into further playlists, crates, and sequences without affecting the 'master' list.

With vinyl, if I were to have a mini set of disco tunes propped up against the leg of my DJ console, I would no longer have any of those tunes in the A to Z on my wall, or in my box for tonight's gig, or in the pile for my new mixtape, because they'd have to have been removed from those places for the purposes of my new playlist idea. But with any decent music library software, including iTunes and your DJ software, you can have multiple instances of any of your tunes going on, so a track could appear in all kinds of playlists while being in your master list too.

Playlists - the digital equivalent of my record boxes and random propped-up piles of tunes that meant something to me - come in two types, so let's look at how you'd use each:

Manual playlists. These are where you manually add each tune to a list (look for 'new playlist' or 'new crate' in iTunes, your music library software, or your DJ software). You drag and drop tunes from somewhere else into such lists. These can be anything: 'Tunes I like right now', 'Possible tunes for Saturday's DJ set', 'New mixtape must-use tunes!', 'Stuff with girl singers', 'Twenty minutes of disco', 'Awesome mini-set'. They can be as permanent or as random as you like (and if you hate clutter, you can nest them too - have a nice, neat folder called 'Random playlists' where you let your creative mind run free and hide it when you want to feel organised). And they're invaluable, because they get ideas out of your head and into your music collection for real, where these ideas can be stored and grow.

Automatic playlists. Often called 'smart playlists' or 'smart crates', these are where you specify certain rules and let the software automatically update the lists with tunes that match those rules as your library grows. These can be useful for things you wish you could do when clicking on columns in your main library, but can't. For instance, once you've sorted by genre to get all your house tunes together, you may then want to sort only the house tunes by year (to arrive at 'all my house tunes from the last year'), which you can't do just by sorting your main list. With smart-type playlists, though, you can; you specify two rules: 'Genre contains house' and 'Added in last twelve months'. These lists are powerful as you can specify endless rules, including and/or operators.

Whenever you start thinking about sequences, or hear tunes that you like together, or want to listen to all the new stuff you've not properly heard yet, or feel the need to OD on 90s house music, or want to hear ten favourite floor-fillers, or need a mellow set for an early morning drive, or are about to play a DJ gig, get into the habit of organising and playlisting that music. Good DJ transitions will come to light. Pairs of tracks will appear, and prove themselves as good fits down the line for your mixing. And when you finally get to pack that all-important crate for a big DJ gig after however many practice sessions, your tracks will feel like a gang of old friends, and at your gig you'll be that DJ, eyes half shut, great song after great song seemingly effortlessly flying out of your collection.

There's just one stage left between your by now well-organised music and DJing with it, and that's analysing it in your DJ software so you can DJ properly with it in your performances. That's what we cover in the next chapter.

Importing Into Your DJ Software

Introduction

When you visit a doctor for the first time, you know how they often give you a clipboard and a whole set of questions to fill in before treating you? They want to know all about your medical history, your allergies, and so on, in order that when you come back next time, you can waltz right in and they can treat you immediately with all of that vital information already on file about you.

When your DJ software sees your music files for the first time, it needs to do something similar. Nowadays, DJ software can help you to achieve some amazing things with your music, but only if it knows some pretty particular stuff about each and every music file first. Just like your doctor, it keeps this information in its own database.

And while you can wait until you actually play each song for this to happen (your software will analyse each track as part of loading it on to a deck in order to find out what it needs to know), it is usually better to bulk analyse new music at the point of importing it into your DJ software.

Why your DJ software needs a library

So what type of good things does your DJ software do for you when you introduce it to your music, and why? Well, boringly, it first makes a copy of a lot of the information already held in the files' ID3 tags (track name, artist, genre, and so on) to allow its own search functions to work well, although it's important to note that it never copies the actual file itself. This stays where you put it (hence the need to be organised). It often analyses the tracks' volumes too to help you have them all the same volume when you're DJing. It is likely to work out the musical key (in order to be able to show you songs that are likely to mix well together harmonically) and will even have a go at guessing where the musical bars or measures lie, along with the tempo, or 'BPM'. All of this is ultimately designed to help you with your mixing.

Once your DJ software has a file entry for each track, it can also remember stuff that *you* have told it about your music. This is typically things like cue points and loops. For instance, if you tell your software a special place in a tune that you always like to start DJing from by setting a cue point, next time you load the track, you can have the software remember that cue point or load with the track ready to play right from that point. This will work even if you turn the software and computer off and on again.

Likewise, as you play more and more sets within your software, it'll glean valuable history information about what you've played, in what order, and when. This is information that can be awesome to have for all types of reasons (there's nothing like looking up what you played last New Year's Eve in your DJ software to give you inspiration for this year, for instance, or basing a DJ set for this week on the mixes that went well last week).

Why it's good to analyse your music in advance

All of this analysing initially takes time and processor power. While DJ software *can* usually cope with seeing a track for the first time while you're actually DJing with it, it puts a strain on your laptop that is inadvisable when performing. Also, analysing in advance gives you the chance to sort and filter your tunes by things like key or BPM before you've even played them in your DJ software. Each type of software has a slightly different method for importing and analysing tracks, but it's always simple to do; just be aware that for larger collections it can take quite a while, so it's a good idea to do it well ahead of time, and keep up to date with it.

It's best not to move your *actual* music files from where they are kept once you've done this. If you do, your DJ software may struggle to find those files because of the fact that it doesn't actually make its own copy of them, just references them. Move the files, and you may find when you next load your software you have a whole list of red 'can't find this track!' warnings. Not good ten minutes before a DJ set...

So when you're ready, grab your particular program's manual, find the section near the front where it talks about importing music, and analyse away.

Where your DJ software stores its information... and why you need to know

It's important to know where your DJ software stores all this info, because this is valuable stuff. If you lose the DJ software's database, you won't lose your actual audio files (because remember the DJ library software doesn't actually *copy* your music files, it just remembers *where* on your system to find them), but you *will* lose all that analysed info, plus any playlists you've made within your DJ software, plus all that good stuff you've told the software about the tracks (cue points, loops, correcting its guesses as to where the beats and bars lie, and so on).

Furthermore, alongside all of this info about your tracks and those software-specific histories and playlists, your DJ software may indeed have *actual audio* somewhere in its own folders, despite the fact that the tunes are stored elsewhere. This could be the output created when you hit 'record' to save a DJ set as you played it, or it could be snippets of songs you've saved as samples within the software to use in your DJing. It could even be whole sample packs that came with your software of useful sounds for you to play with to add texture and excitement to DJ sets.

For all of these reasons, your DJ software's folders are important. Take some time to check your DJ software's manual to find out where it stores this information, and back it up regularly.

And that's it for the music step. In the next section, we'll cover all the DJing techniques you need to know in order to be able to use your gear properly.

Step Three: Techniques

In this step, you'll learn everything you need to know to use your DJ gear and software competently. I'll show you the basic DJing workflow, and then explain in detail how your mixer and decks work, talk you through beatmixing, and reveal an essential set of transition techniques to get you through practically any DJ set. I'll also give you an insight into using some of the bells and whistles of modern DJ gear, including sync, hot cues, loops, EQ, filter, and effects. Plus, I'll show you the most effective way to critique your DJ sets so you improve fast.

The Basic DJing Technique

Introduction

In my long career as a professional DJ, I've dealt with all types of people begging to be in the DJ booth with me. From old friends wanting to escape the packed dancefloor for a bit, to girls looking for somewhere to dance where they will be seen more by everyone else, to other DJs wanting to chat or - worse - look through my music, there always seemed to be someone keen on joining me.

But while I was generally pretty harsh on people who, as I saw it, wanted to invade my workspace, there was a certain type for whom I often caved in. He (for it was nearly always a he) used to approach the booth and ask quietly, 'Do you mind if I come in and watch what you're doing you for a bit? I won't say anything, or get in your way...'

The physical movements, the actual process of DJing, is both a mystery and a fascination to those who don't yet know the sequence of steps. The good news is that the steps are remarkably similar no matter what DJ gear is involved. It's like driving: sure, driving a small city car is different to driving a luxury automatic 4x4, which is different to driving a container truck, but the similarities far outweigh the differences.

This chapter blows the lid on the basic technique. Here I'm going to talk you through what DJs are actually doing when they play a DJ set - step by step. Remember your first ever driving lesson, where clutch and hand brake and accelerator and ignition and steering wheel and indicators all blurred into one unknowable mess, only to slowly make sense as you had them all explained to you methodically and took your first spin around the block? This chapter is the DJ version of that.

Happy driving...

Step-by-step: what a DJ actually does

1. Find and load the next tune. Get the tune you want to play next on to an unused deck, making sure that deck is not live (i.e. its faders are closed). Route that tune's audio to your headphones by pressing its 'Pre-fader listen', 'Headphones' or 'Cue' button.

2. Prepare the tune for playing. That means setting the channel gain so the tune isn't too quiet, or distorting; checking its EQ (to make sure there's not too much or too little bass, and it doesn't sound too muddy or harsh, for example); getting its tempo right; and picking the place you want to play it from, cueing it up at that point (usually a downbeat or what I call a 'one beat', which just means the first significant beat of a section).

3. Test the transition. This is like a dress rehearsal for the transition you'll be doing for real soon enough. Waiting until a good place in the current track, you get the tune playing. Then, with one ear listening to the speakers or booth monitors (that are playing the current tune out loud), and the other ear listening to your headphones (that are playing the new tune privately - hence the DJ look with a hand holding a single headphone cup to a single ear), you make any small adjustments to tempo, while at the same time deciding for sure if you've made the right choice of tune. If not, you go back to step one and try again with something else.

4. Begin the transition. Returning the tune to your chosen 'in' or 'cue' point, you start it playing over the top of the current tune, effectively repeating step three, but for the final 'real' time.

5. Make the new tune live. This means turning its levels up so your audience can finally hear it too. This could be at exactly the same time as the previous stage, or it could be a few beats, bars or a whole musical phrase or two later, with you monitoring in your headphones in the meantime.

6. Perform the transition. Depending on the type of transition you're doing, here's where you manage the two tunes as they play together, using the levels and tone controls of one or both of them to move your audience's attention from one tune to the next. When beatmixing, this stage can go on for several musical phrases; with many types of mixes, it is very short, and for one type of mix, it is non-existent (when you cut straight from one tune to the next).

7. Stop the outgoing tune playing. When the transition is totally over, you stop the old tune playing. Its deck is now the unused deck.

8. Return to step one.

Just like driving a car, it's not actually the steps themselves but how smoothly you enact them that really counts here.

Now you have a sense of the overall sequence of DJing track to track, for the rest of this step, we'll look at all the things you need to know to do the above successfully, starting in the next chapter by looking at your mixer.

Understanding Your Mixer

Introduction

Every DJ set-up has some kind of mixer. A mixer does three things: firstly, as you may guess, it lets you mix the different elements of your DJ set together. Usually these are two music sources, but they could include a microphone or two, a back-up music source, a live bongo player…be our guest. Something's got to take all of these inputs and give you one unified output that can be amplified and sent to the speakers. That'd be your mixer.

Secondly, your mixer lets you adjust the volumes of those inputs, and often the tone as well (bass and treble, or lows and highs, at a minimum for the main inputs – there's often a mid as well which sits between the two, giving you three tone controls at least for the main input channels). There will always be an overall volume control, too.

Thirdly (and crucially for DJing), your mixer lets you play something different through your headphones to what the crowd is hearing. To DJ well, you have to be able to audition the next track to decide for sure that it's what you want to use, to get its volume and tone settings right *before* the audience hears it, and to get it playing at the right speed, the last point being an essential part of the DJ skill of beatmixing.

A hardware DJ mixer, in this case, the Allen & Heath Xone:43. The basic controls are the same on any size or type of mixer, including those in DJ software.

Physically, a mixer usually sits between your input sources. So nowadays in a pro DJ booth, you'll typically see a four channel mixer (so called because it has four main inputs, plus various microphones, auxiliary inputs, etc.) sitting between a pair or more of DJ media players (think CD players with extra bells and whistles). Of course, the classic DJ set-up is a pair of vinyl turntables with a hardware mixer sitting between them.

With DJ software, this mixer is generally portrayed onscreen positioned between two or more decks, just as described above, and the actual mixing occurs inside your computer itself (usually controlled via some kind of DJ hardware, such as a DJ controller, plugged into the computer), although it is possible to use your computer effectively as a pair of digital decks, feeding two outputs into an external mixer like with more traditional gear.

Dial up 'DJ mixer' in Google Images and you could be forgiven for feeling overwhelmed by the plethora of knobs and buttons. Likewise if your DJ software is one that can display a DJ mixer onscreen for you, which again invariably looks complicated. But once you understand the elements at play, it becomes simple. So let's look more closely at those elements:

Channels

Every mixer has a number of channels. You hear phrases like 'two channel mixer' and 'four channel mixer' and can easily identify the main channels by looking for sets of controls that repeat each other, laid out vertically.

Each channel is simply a set of controls to alter things about the input it is fed. A channel will nearly always have the following:

A gain control (also called 'trim') – a volume knob that can raise or lower the volume of the input before anything else is done to it.

EQ or equalisation controls – these are your bass, mid, and treble knobs for making the overall tone of the input sound good, and for smooth mixing.

A main channel volume control – a fader to decide how much of the channel's output goes into the overall mix.

Channels often have meters to show you visually how loud they are too (this is where the phrase 'keep it out of the red' comes from, as the final bar or bars on a level or VU meter are usually red coloured, and indicate the music is too loud). Channels may also have some kind of dedicated effects, such as a filter control (filter is like a super-musical tone control), or maybe a reverb or echo effect if it's a microphone channel (makes the microphone sound more professional).

Routing controls

Once your sources are at the right volume and all sound great, you're going to need to control how they blend together. You've already learned about one control to do that, the main channel volume control for each channel. Push more than one of these vertical faders up, and you'll hear more than one music source together. Some mixers stop right there. But most of today's mixers, whether actual hardware or within your DJ software, usually have a crossfader (the little horizontal fader at the bottom of a mixer) that lets you cut quickly between assigned musical inputs - an essential part of scratch mixing.

Other routing controls on a mixer may include an input matrix, which lets you select between multiple inputs for each of the mixer's channels, controls for DJ effects, either built in to the mixer or plugged in separately, and multiple output controls, so you can decide how loud the signals are that you send to the main speakers and to your booth output (where you'd plug in speakers that are meant only for the DJ booth).

Headphones controls

These are really just another routing option, but they deserve their own explanation because of how crucial they are to DJing. Each channel on a DJ mixer will have a cue button (sometimes called pre-fade listen or PFL). When switched on, this will send that channel's output to your headphones. It won't change the amount of that channel, if any, currently going to the master output one bit - it'll just decide whether what's going on in that channel is sent to your headphones *in addition*. In some mixers, you can only send one channel to the headphones at one time, but in most, you can toggle all or any of them on or off. This is how you get to audition an input before you choose to add it to the mix of what your crowd is hearing.

Just like with the main mix, the headphones mix also has a volume control of its own so you can adjust how loud your headphones are, and this channel may have additional controls too (a typical one is a cue mix that lets you blend together what the audience is hearing with what is being sent to your headphones).

However the mixer is set up in your DJ system, the important things are that you know how to get your music playing through it, how to hear each source in your headphones independently, and how to move from one source to another on your main speakers. If you haven't worked this out yet on your particular DJ gear, now's the time to do so before we move on to look at the decks themselves, which is where you'll learn how to control your music sources properly.

Understanding Your Decks

Introduction

Over at my website Digital DJ Tips, we have taught thousands of DJs to 'scratch'. The skills of scratching involve rhythmic manipulation of the music, which in the case of DJs using today's equipment is usually done via their equipment's jogwheels rather than using real vinyl. One thing we've found is that we have to train DJs starting out today to get over the feeling that they shouldn't be touching the music in this way; that they'll somehow get found out; that it will sound terrible; that they might *break something*.

Well the truth is, as a DJ you absolutely must get comfortable with touching the music. You need to be grabbing hold of the jogwheels or platters. You need to develop a healthy curiosity for what things sound like when you use all the controls at your disposal to stop and start your music, and alter the music's default state of simply playing from A to B. Imagine the track on your deck to be a car. You've got to grab the wheel and drive that baby!

How it's done with vinyl

Let's return for a minute to the days of turntables and real vinyl, because even the most modern DJ controllers usually use this paradigm as their starting point.

A DJ turntable, in this case the Reloop RP7000. The disc with the logo on it is called a 'slipmat', and allows the DJ fine control over the music, slipping when the DJ pauses the track by touching the vinyl as the motor continues to turn.

You may be surprised to learn that the first thing a vinyl DJ puts on a turntable when he or she wants to play a record is not, well, a record. No, it's a slipmat, which is a thin record-shaped piece of felt-like material. When the record is placed on top of it, the slipmat reduces the resistance between the spinning platter and the piece of vinyl. This means that if the DJ touches the edge of the spinning tune, the vinyl stops moving, but the platter carries on spinning underneath as if nothing has happened. When he or she takes their hand off the record, it gets up to speed again pretty quickly. With a slipmat in place, a turntable becomes a sensitive music manipulation device, giving the DJ the chance to pause, start, scratch, and rewind any record with precision. Grab the vinyl firmly enough and you can even spin the record backwards, until inertia brings it back to playing as it should.

The traditions above are carried on today with digital vinyl systems (DVSs). You'll recall a DVS is a kit that can convert any turntable set-up into a digital DJ system using special control or timecode vinyl that feels like the real thing, but actually contains computer code that can talk to DJ software, letting the DJ play digital music with existing gear.

A modern DJ deck, in this case, the Pioneer DJ CDJ2000NXS2. The decks built in to all-in-one DJ controllers have the same features described here.

When record decks were largely replaced with CD decks (and later DJ controllers), out went real decks, slipmats and vinyl, and in came jogwheels. While jogwheels do occasionally come with motors, slipmats and imitation vinyl to ape the feel of turntables, manufacturers quickly realised that this wasn't necessary to give DJs the control they needed, and so the vast majority of jogwheels on DJ equipment are static. This is not in the sense that they're fixed, but more in the sense that they don't go around when you hit play any more. Apart from that, though, the way they behave is similar to turntables.

Manufacturers figured out that, when manipulating a piece of music, DJs basically do two distinct things. The first is 'grabbing the track' to stop it, hold it where it is, scratch it, rewind it, or do any other drastic action with it. The second is very different, and involves subtly nudging the tune momentarily faster or slower, almost always in order to keep it playing in time with something else. 'As long as we can let DJs do both of these things,' the manufacturers reasoned, 'we can build all the functionality of a big, heavy motor-driven turntable into a small inches-wide static jogwheel.'

The way the manufacturers did it was by making the top surface of the jogwheel work in scratch mode (touch it and hold it and the music will stop; move your hand backwards and the track will go backwards at the speed your hand is moving; let go and it'll carry on playing from there), and the edge of the jogwheel work in nudge mode (nothing happens when you touch it, but when you nudge it clockwise the track speeds up slightly until your movement stops, and when you move the jogwheel backwards, the track slows down momentarily).

When you see DJ gear - from kit in pro DJ booths all the way down to cheap home DJ controllers - with something round and bigger than the rest of the controls on it, but that isn't a turntable, that something is called a jogwheel, and it nearly always behaves as described above. Jogwheels are uncannily good at giving DJs the vinyl feel without the weight, expense, and complication.

From jogwheels to touchstrips

A touchstrip DJ deck, in this case, the Traktor Kontrol D2.
Notice the horizontal strip that replaces the platter or
jogwheel from the other types of deck, although in use,
the function it performs is the same.

This idea of manipulating your music by rotating something has been at the heart of DJing for so many decades, it's hard to separate it from what DJing is. But there's nothing to say it is an intrinsic part of DJing, any more than vinyl itself is (it clearly isn't, as nowadays most DJs don't use or even own any vinyl). So while most DJ gear does indeed still have something round on it to help you control the music, some doesn't.

The latest development of the jogwheel is called a touchstrip. When you swipe your smartphone, you essentially perform the action a touchstrip lets you perform.

Imagine a strip, about the size of a nail file, designed to let you control your music. You can perform the nudge functions described above by swiping your finger on it, one direction to speed the track up, one to slow it down. Sometimes, there's a toggle switch nearby that lets you switch the touchstrip into scratch mode for the other type of movement.

So now, on a control no larger than a pen, it's possible to do much of what you can do on a full-sized motorised turntable. And if you're wondering, yes, you can scratch on a touchstrip - we've done the experiments! We wouldn't recommend it, though…

The transport controls

Back in the days of cassette tape players, the transport parts were the parts the tape passed through, and when you pressed the play button, the transport physically moved to engage with the tape. The word has persisted, so today we use transport to talk about controls like play, pause, stop, and so on for our DJ decks.

While on a record deck all you get is start and stop, on DJ players with jogwheels or touchstrips, you usually get a few more controls. The most important one is play/pause. Touch this once, and the track starts. Touch again, and it pauses. Touch again, it starts from where it was paused. No surprises there, then. It is almost always alongside a button marked 'cue'. This button adds a temporary cue point to the track, usually used to mark where you want to start your track playing from.

Here's how this button works: with the track paused, you use the jogwheel to manipulate the track until, say, immediately before the very first beat of the track (often a good bet for where to start it playing). Then you press the cue point button to mark that point. Now, when the track is playing, you can jump back to the cue point by simply touching the cue point button.

Taken together, these two buttons - combined with using the jogwheel or touchstrip - give you all the manipulation of your music you're ever likely to need, putting you in the driver's seat of your mix.

So, armed with a working knowledge of your DJ mixer from the previous chapter and your DJ decks from this chapter, you're ready to turn to that DJs' holy grail, the science of beatmixing. That's what the next two chapters tackle.

Beatmixing Part 1: Timing

Introduction

When I was a kid, I bought a paperback book called *The DJ's Handbook - From Scratch To Stardom* by Roy Sheppard. Predating DJ CD players, never mind digital DJing, it taught things like how to build cassette decks and kit-assembled turntables into carpeted coffin cases, how to conduct dancefloor drinking games, and the best way to deal with hecklers. But tucked among those essential skills was this:

> If a DJ is very skilled he can play or 'run' both records simultaneously for some time before fading one of them out. Performed properly it is difficult if not impossible to tell where one record ends and another begins, but bad mixes are noticed very easily.

The glamour of those fifty words in a 200-page book lodged itself instantly in my mind, and of course this kind of DJing has become a core skill in the decades that have followed. I certainly wouldn't blame you if you've turned to this chapter right on picking up this book.

But if you're still not sure what it means, beatmixing describes having your tracks playing at the same BPM (beats per minute), otherwise known as speed or tempo, blending them smoothly together, their rhythms tightly locked. It's a great technique to help with playing smooth, accomplished DJ sets. DJs often feel they're going to be judged on their ability to do it, and it's true that people certainly spot bad beatmixing pretty quickly ('This DJ keeps train-crashing!').

A word of warning, though: the truth is that if you want to play DJ sets that fill dancefloors, get you booked again, and let you play the music you want to play, you need to put beatmixing in its rightful place. It is a single technique for smoothly moving from one song to the next that works in some circumstances and doesn't in others. That said, DJs can either beatmix or they can't, and like the teenage me, I'm sure you want to be one of those who can. Just don't let beatmixing rule your DJing - remember that the right music, in the right order, for the people in front of you right now will always trump *any* specific technique.

What's this about timing?

I mention timing in the chapter title not to remind you to play the next record at the right time of night (that'd be *programming*), or because I want to talk about *where* in the playing track you start to move to the next track (which is more part of your DJing style, and will depend on the type of music you're playing among other things). No, timing refers to knowing how to maintain the flow of the music when beatmixing, so that elements of the two tracks you're lining up obey basic musical rules.

Without the right timing, beatmixing counts for nothing.

Practically all music that any DJ will ever want to beatmix with obeys certain musical rules. One of those is that there are *four beats in a bar*. (You may hear a 'bar' called a 'measure', but the words mean the same thing.) Try this: put a dance tune on and start counting out loud '*One*, two, three, four' repeatedly over the 'thud, thud, thud, thud' of the bass (or kick) drum. Emphasise the one as you do. You'll soon see that dance music is arranged in groups of four beats - bars. These four-beat bars are the basic building blocks of pretty much all tracks, a truth acknowledged in the phrase 'four to the floor' to describe dance music. If you're beatmixing and you line up your beats but not your bars, it's going to sound awful.

In musical notation, this is what four beats in a bar looks like.

However, while lining up your ones, twos, threes and fours is certainly a good first step, music is built around bigger patterns than that. Track intros, verses, choruses, breakdowns, bridges and drops - in other words, every part of every track, from start to finish, is built around groups of bars, which we will call musical phrases.

A pop song may go intro, verse, chorus, verse, chorus, bridge, chorus, outro. (The 'bridge' is the linking bit with a different melody before the final chorus.) A dance track may not really have choruses, but may have a single phrase that repeats over and over again building up to a breakdown (drum-less section) and riser (same bit but with tension-building elements coming in) followed by the hallowed drop (where it all goes crazy). Different genres, different arrangements – but they are all built around groups of bars, and the thing to remember is that these are nearly always groups of four or eight, often referred to by DJs as 'phrases'. This single fact is the key to unlocking accomplished beatmixing.

I am about to share with you two things that will teach you all you need to know about this musical side of beatmixing. Neither of these will ever leave you, but many DJs don't work out this stuff:

Count in phrases, and always be counting. When you're beatmixing two tracks, if you can line up *phrases* in your tracks, and not just beats and bars, you'll be way ahead of the pack. That's why DJs are *always* counting beats and bars. We don't always do it out loud, but we do it. And in order to count phrases, not just bars, successfully, we don't go '*One*, two, three, four, *one*, two, three, four', either. Try this instead: to count a four-bar phrase, count, '*One*, two, three, four, *two*, two, three, four, *three*, two, three, four, *four*, two, three, four'. Then, return to '*One*, two, three, four'. (You don't need me to tell you how to count an eight-bar phrase, right?) You'll notice that the *one* beat, or downbeat, is where stuff happens - a verse starts, a chorus starts, the drop starts, elements leave the track, a vocal begins, a new synth line or percussive element arrives or an old one leaves, and so on. All songs are built around these structures - your job when mixing is to be counting along.

Map a few songs out on paper. Nothing will help you understand how the music you love is structured into musical phrases like mapping it out on paper, and doing this will clear the clouds on why some beatmixes work and some don't as your DJing progresses. Take a piece of squared paper and turn it width-ways, and let each square represent four or eight bars. Now, counting through a track and pausing when you need to, from the start, write into the sets of four or eight bars what each part of the track is. Don't worry about whether your choice of words is right - you may write 'intro', 'intro with beat', 'intro with louder beat', 'vocal bit', 'vocal bit again', 'no beat section', 'drop' - the wording really doesn't matter. The point is that you learn to break a whole track down into four or eight bar sections or phrases. As you map out a handful of tracks, you'll start to get a feel for how pretty much all music - at least, all music you're likely to want to DJ with - is constructed from exactly these types of building blocks, or phrases, of bars.

Once you can count along in this way with a playing track, the next part of your job as a beatmixing DJ is to start another track playing over the top of the current one so that its musical phrases (its '*one*, two, three, four, *two*, two, three, four...') line up with the current track. The next chapter will show you exactly what's needed to get that right.

Beatmixing Part 2: The Three Elements Of A Good Beatmix

Introduction

DJs often use the phrases 'beatmatching' and 'beatmixing' interchangeably, and that's fine, but I find it useful to be a bit more precise in our wording. Let's call a beatmix the overall technique, of which beatmatching is one of the three elements you need to get right for your beatmix to work. The other two are phrase matching (lining up your musical phrases, which we talked about in the previous chapter) and tempo matching, which is where we'll start.

Tempo matching

Beatmixing, as we now know, is partly about lining up two tracks so their beats lock together, neither track playing faster than the other. In order for this to work, the speed, or BPM, or tempo of each track must match. Tempo matching, then, is the very first thing that has to happen for a beatmix to work.

Ever since the introduction of DJ CD players, modern DJ equipment has had BPM counters built in. These show you the BPM of each track. By adjusting the pitch control (it's usually a fader, but it can be a knob), a DJ can alter the speed of a track and thus alter the BPM readout. The game is to get the speeds of the two sources you want to beatmix so that they're the same before attempting the mix. Dance music can range from 80BPM for the slowest hip hop jams right up past 120 (house) to 180 (drum & bass), but it is always best to beatmix tunes whose BPMs are pretty close anyway, and a good rule of thumb is plus or minus 4%. So for house, that means looking for tunes around 5BPM either side of the one you're currently playing to beatmix with. (By the way, BPM readouts didn't always exist, and still don't on most record decks - vinyl DJs often count BPMs with a stopwatch and attach stickers to their tunes showing the BPM to help them to plan their beatmixes, or simply do it by feel.)

Beatmatching

It's not enough, though, to have the speeds set the same. Once they are, it is then necessary for the beats themselves to line up correctly. You need the 'thud, thud, thud' of the main drums that are driving your songs forward to line up too.

Imagine you're playing a house track with four main beats per bar, and you have another track at exactly the same speed, but playing a bit ahead of the first one - now you'll have an unholy mess. Instead of the four beats in each bar playing at exactly the same time as each other, and effectively merging into one beat, they are all audible individually, so you can hear eight beats where there should only be four. With beatmixing, we're trying to move from track to track without the audience noticing, but clearly if we introduce an extra set of beats out of nowhere that isn't in line with the existing beats, it's going to be instantly noticeable and simply sound wrong (remember that train-wrecking I mentioned earlier?). So as well as our songs being tempo matched, they need to be beatmatched.

Phrase matching

The whole of the previous chapter was about how the tracks you love are constructed in mathematically predictable musical phrases, so you already know what this requirement is all about. If you've jumped to here without reading the previous chapter, you've skipped a vital part – go and catch up before going any further.

Remember the counting system from the previous chapter – the 'one, two, three, four, *two*, two, three four…' method of counting blocks of typically four or eight bars in a track? In practical terms, phrase matching means that as well as the beats being the same speed and lined up, the sets of 'one, two, three, four, *two*, two, three, four…' in each track are lined up, too. The easiest way to do this when beatmixing is to have your incoming track ready to go on a *one* beat at the start of the phrase where you want to begin playing it, and start playing it when the outgoing track reaches a *one* beat too, so the phrases are lined up nicely. We call that first beat at the start of a phrase the 'one beat', or the 'downbeat'.

How to perform a beatmix

Hopefully you're starting to see how it fits together now. You just have to get the BPM counters showing the same speed (tempo) and start the second track playing over the first, making sure the downbeats are lined up, and that one track isn't slightly ahead of or behind the other, so you don't accidentally double up the number of main beats audible instead of having them neatly laid over the top of each other.

But it's not quite so simple. As not all DJ systems have BPM readouts, and not all tracks have a reliable constant BPM (you're usually good with electronic music, but anything played by a real drummer is going to vary a bit - think funk, disco, rock and so on), even when you think you have your BPMs set right, they may slip apart over time. That's why it is important to know how to beatmix manually - get two tracks playing at the same speed and know how to keep them there without the need for automatic BPM counters and other beatmixing tools. It's one of those skills, like riding a bike, that comes in the end and won't leave you once it does, but to get there you do need to keep at it.

Here's how to do it. Practising using simple house music with a strong beat is good, and using two copies of the same track helps, too. Extra points for covering your BPM readouts!

1. With the first track playing, have the second ready with your cue point on a *one* beat, its speed set at any old rough

guess, or simply middle, on the pitch fader. The best *one* beat is often the very first beat of the track.

2. When you reach a *one* beat on the first track, start the second track playing (you do this so you can only hear it in your headphones when performing, but it's fine to do it all in the loudspeakers when practising, i.e. with both tracks playing out loud).

3. Unless you're lucky, the new track will either be too slow or too fast, and you'll hear it pull away from or fall behind the main track. Use your cue button to get it back to the *one* beat or the start, adjust the pitch control up or down a bit, and try again.

4. Go back to 2 and repeat until the tracks are taking a while to pull apart, which means their BPMs are getting close.

5. At this stage, instead of going back to the beginning to make your adjustments, you can nudge the incoming track using the platter or jogwheel. This means using your hand on the platter, jogwheel or vinyl to speed it up or slow it down momentarily when you hear the beats slipping apart in order to line them up again. Once they're lined up, you make a small adjustment to the pitch control to get even closer to the real matching BPM. Eventually, you'll have it spot on so the tracks stay perfectly lined up for as long as you need to perform a smooth mix between them using the mixer. In a real DJ set, you'd have done all of this preparation in your headphones, and you'd then go right back to the start and do it live over the speakers.

Practise, practise, practise...

If the above sounds a little tricky, I won't dress it up: it is. At first, you don't think you'll ever get it. You certainly feel that it won't ever be possible to do it fast enough. But you will, and you can. Practised DJs learn how to skip steps three and four, starting a track playing and, by a deft few nudges and tempo control adjustments, getting two tunes lined up manually in a few seconds.

It really doesn't matter what gear or system you're using, either. Obviously, turn off or don't use any auto sync functions. Look for functions called 'snap' or 'quantise' if you're using DJ software, and avoid or turn those off too. And on CDJs and DJ software, as I said, you can cover up the BPM counters to force you to work out by ear which track is playing the faster of the two in your mixes (use Post-it notes on your CD displays or laptop screen to hide the BPMs).

If you're struggling, just remember what I said at the beginning of the previous chapter: beatmixing is a single technique for smoothly moving from one song to the next. It's not even appropriate in a lot of circumstances, and it needn't hold you back from performing live and enjoying your DJing. Indeed, in the next chapter, we move on to actual real-life DJ transitions…and only two of the five I'm about to show you use beatmixing at all.

Five Basic DJ Transitions

Introduction

Here's the dirty truth about how to DJ. If this were a book about an exciting new type of cuisine, this would be the secret sauce mix. If it were a book for wannabe bartenders about mixing cocktails, it'd be the five must-have ingredients and the trick to shaking properly. But it's not: it's about DJing, and the techniques in this chapter are truly the only ones you need to be able to play music continuously and professionally for people to dance to.

Of course, knowing a secret sauce or two doesn't make you a world-class chef, just like mastering a few cocktails doesn't turn you into The Savoy's next cocktail mixologist. What follows won't get you to the DMC World DJ Championships - but these DJ transitions are the building blocks for everything. Combined with good ingredients (your music), confidence in your tools (your DJ gear), and a clear idea about what you're aiming for (filling that dancefloor at the next gig you've got in your diary), they will get you on the field of play.

Once you've mastered the five techniques here, you'll be in the enviable position of not worrying about *how* you're going to mix from one tune to the next (so you can worry about what matters: *what* to play next), and you'll naturally start developing your style by adding your own flavours to these techniques. Like cooking and cocktail making, once you know the basics, there are countless variations, and soon enough you'll not only be able to come up with your own ideas, but you'll better understand and appreciate what other DJs are doing too…and be able to borrow some of their techniques for your own DJ sets.

Transition #1: the Fade

Most songs don't actually fade at the end any more, something that used to be the norm. The last fade I can recall on a recent pop song was Robin Thicke's 2013 hit 'Blurred Lines' - maybe you can think of more. Yet as a DJ tool, the Fade remains one of the best ways to move from song to song in a DJ set. It is your 'get out of jail' card. Knowing how to fade and move on means you'll never be stuck for a way to move to the next tune, and the confidence that gives you is priceless.

Manually fading a song out tells the audience the current track is ending and to expect something else imminently, and of course removes a lot of the volume from the outgoing tune so that the moment the incoming tune starts, it dominates. Done smoothly and confidently, the Fade puts control of where you switch from one tune to the next into your hands, and tells everyone you're in command. Combined with good timing, it's a perfectly acceptable way to move along in many types of DJ set.

How to do it

1. Decide where you want to fade. At times, you will do this because you played the wrong song and want to move on apologetically (hey, it happens), but usually it'll be because you feel you've played enough of something that hasn't quite ended yet, which is common especially when you're playing older music that everyone knows. A chorus is a good place to fade, or even better, a chorus that follows a chorus (a common way writers pad out their songs towards the end). If that second chorus is also introduced by a key change (that other classic 'running out of ideas' composition technique), all the better.

2. Fade the song out quickly at first, then slowly. The wrong way to fade a song out is to make people ask, 'Is this or isn't this fading out?' You've got to be bold and knock a good chunk of that volume out right away. Over the next ten to fifteen seconds, you can continue the Fade more gradually, now everyone's clear what's going on. If you start your fade just after the beginning of, say, an eight-bar musical phrase, you'll want to be practically done with it by the end of that phrase so you can…

3. Start the next track playing on a downbeat, lined up with the final downbeat on your outgoing track. Just as your old track is disappearing, hit play on your new track, crisply and cleanly lined up right on the first beat of a musical phrase. Doesn't matter if it's an actual beat or not, just ensure that you're at the start of a phrase so you respect the flow of the tracks together.

Also, it doesn't matter if the track is of a different BPM, or even a different genre, a fact that makes the Fade a great way to help you play more interesting sets that confidently cross genres and tempos.

Bonus: watch a video demonstrating this technique at http://djtips.co/transition1

Transition #2: the End-to-End

All you've got to do is listen to music radio for long enough to get a decent handle on the End-to-End. This simple mixing style is very much of today, with our modern fashion for short, choppy pop, dance and hip hop singles that start with a bang and end just as abruptly. This style of music doesn't lend itself necessarily to anything more than a confident switch from one tune to the next. Like anything simple, though, its mechanics are laid bare for all to see, and to get this one right requires more skill than you might imagine.

How to do it

1. **Know how the current song is going to end.** Firstly, you need to be sure that there is indeed a nice clean ending there for you to work with. Examining the waveform on your screen can help, but when push comes to shove, I've been known to load another copy of the current song on to a spare deck while the first one is playing to my audience and have a quick listen in my headphones to find out how it ends (ah,

the joys of digital, where double copies of anything can be so simple). Once you're sure about that...

2. Choose a strong, impactful next song with an immediate starting point. No point boldly switching from the very end of one song into a whimpering slow-starting nothing kind of tune, no matter how great it is once it gets going. You need something that starts with a bang. (Notice how on radio there are often edited versions of songs that do precisely that, or the DJ starts the song playing where it gets going rather than where it really starts in its full meandering version. You might want to think about doing that, too.)

When you're asking your audience to deal with such a big, bold switch as this, it helps if they are likely to be accepting of the new song immediately, so recognisable is always good.

3. Count the beats and bars as the outgoing song ends, and start the new song playing on a downbeat, making sure that your new song has its fader up so it's audible, of course. It's important to note that respecting the musical flow is the secret sauce that binds this kind of apparently random mix together and ultimately lets you get away with it. Counting your 'one, two, three, four, two, two, three, four...' beats and bars leading up to where you start the new song playing on both its and the outgoing tune's downbeat is the key. If the outgoing tune stops in a truly random place (which is unlikely), meaning you can't start the new tune at the beginning of a new four- or eight-bar phrase, at least start it on the first beat of a bar, counting in your head past the end of the tune and leaving a small amount of silence if you have to.

Bonus: watch a video demonstrating this technique at http://djtips.co/transition2

Transition #3: the Cut

Manchester, England, late 1980s. I was barely old enough to go clubbing, but nevertheless used to roll up at a club called Legend on Princess Street, a place known for its unbelievable light show, huge sound system, and the quality of its DJs. (It was the venue featured in the video for the song 'Wrote For Luck' by Madchester band Happy Mondays, if you want to check it out on YouTube.)

This was just before the big UK acid house revolution of 1988, when the first wave of electronic dance music changed club culture forever, so nobody really knew what beatmixing was at the time. Yet the resident DJ was mixing flawlessly, everything from indie to hip hop to sixties psychedelia, most of it from 7-inch singles. His name was Dave Booth (one of the unsung heroes of my home city's often celebrated club scene), and the techniques he'd use all night long to keep his floors packed were the two I've already covered, and the Cut.

Unlike the End-to-End and the Fade, both of which have signalled to your audience that something is about to happen before it actually does (the first because the song is ending, the second because it's disappearing), the Cut is a momentary instant mix – a clean cut from one track to the next that relies for its power on three things: timing (as ever), your choice of *where* in both of your tracks to do it, and the actual tracks you've chosen in the first place. Get these things right and, like Dave Booth at Legend all those decades ago and countless multi-genre, multi-tempo DJs since, you can quite happily mix all night with this and the other techniques you've learned so far.

How to do it

1. Line your incoming track up on a one beat. You need to be able to start this track instantly at the millisecond of your choosing right at the start of a musical phrase, so pick your *one* beat (see 'Beatmixing Part 1: Timing' for more information about *one* beats) and get it ready.

2. Start counting the beats, bars, and phrases on your outgoing track. You're looking for a corresponding *one* beat where if the track you have lined up were to take over, it would all sound good. Typically, you're looking for a part of the track towards the end where things are winding down, and the big verses, choruses, breakdowns, drops, hooks, etc. are being removed from the mix by the producer, so there's a building sense that something else is coming at some point.

3. On your chosen downbeat, start your new track playing, and immediately stop the outgoing one. You're effectively switching from one song to the next while continuing the natural flow of beats, bars, and phrases, i.e. going from a '...*three*, two three, four, *four*, two, three four' on your outgoing tune back to '*one*, two, three four...', but the second the *one* hits, your old tune has gone and the new tune has taken over.

Exactly how you do the above will of course depend on your equipment. Dave used to use real vinyl and physically throw the new song in on time, but with modern gear, you simply hit the stop button on one deck while hitting the start button on the other – making sure the incoming tune is fully faded up in the mix, of course.

Bonus: watch a video demonstrating this technique at http://djtips.co/transition3

Transition #4: the Single Phrase Beatmix

And so we come back to beatmixing, a core DJ skill so important that, to many observers of the DJ scene, it – alongside scratching – *is* DJing. Master this and the following beatmixed transition, and everyone will be convinced of your DJing chops, including all other DJs. (If you find the beatmixing parts simply too hard, in the next chapter you'll learn how you can use your gear's 'sync' function, if it offers one, to make it much easier.)

As always, the key is in timing and programming as much as in the techniques themselves, but once you are sure you've picked the right tune to play next, and you're sensing it's time to make that switch with a nice beatmix, here are a couple of time-tested techniques, beloved of DJs the world over. We'll start with the Single Phrase Beatmix, so called because you play both tunes together for one musical phrase, usually of four or eight bars.

How to do it

1. Prepare the incoming tune for a beatmix (as per the 'Beatmixing' chapters). Usually this will be somewhere near the start, at a section where there are just drums. Line this tune up one musical phrase *before* the place you'd like to make it audible to your audience, giving you a bit of lead in.

2. Start it playing in your headphones over the outgoing tune. Do this exactly as if you were doing the Cut, i.e. completely lined up with a *one* beat. Because the tempo of the incoming tune has been set to the same as the outgoing tune, as long as you started it at the right time (or used your DJ software's sync feature if that's how you DJ to ensure the same), the beats will be perfectly in time; if they're not, you know how to correct this from the 'Beatmixing' chapter.

3. After your one musical phrase lead in, make the new tune audible to your audience over the top of the outgoing one. That initial phrase where you listened to the new tune in your headphones only was for you to double check it was lined up and sounded good, so now it does, on this *one* beat, introduce it to your audience. Usually this is done by putting the crossfader to the middle, or if it's already there (or you don't use it or have one), bringing the tune's channel line fader up so the music is playing through the speakers.

4. Play the tunes together for a musical phrase. This will be for four, often eight, sometimes even sixteen bars, depending on the two tunes, but the point is to let your audience hear the thrill of two tunes perfectly lined up playing together for a meaningful musical length of time - a phrase being the minimum length that signifies this.

5. Mix out the outgoing tune. Now it's time to retire the old track, and so you'll move the crossfader all the way across, or bring down its line fader, or whatever. You can do this in one go on the downbeat, or slowly fade it out; as long as it stays nicely lined up and there's nothing clashing between the two tracks (usually discordant melodies, an eventuality you avoid by mixing where only drums dominate), frankly it's down to you.

It's easy to turn this into a double phrase beatmix or more by keeping those tunes playing together for longer. However, having two full bass drums thumping away together in your mix at the same time, and any accompanying basslines and other musical information that may be arriving or leaving the mix too, could sound muddy and messy. That's where the next transition really comes into its own.

Bonus: watch a video demonstrating this technique at http://djtips.co/transition4

Transition #5: the Bassline Swap Beatmix

Ever seen a DJ jumping around in the booth, highly animated, yet with both hands firmly fixed to the mixer? On closer inspection, he or she appears to have the finger and thumb of each hand grasping a single knob...and at just the right moment, with one dual exaggerated twist of those two knobs, our hero propels the room into the next tune. Cue an amazing reaction from the crowd, etc., etc.

More than likely, what you witnessed the DJ doing right there was the Bassline Swap Beatmix. For certain types of music (think house, techno, trance, modern disco), this is the go-to mix that millions of DJs use night after night to play smooth, musically tight sets. And once you can do the Single Phrase Beatmix, it's a simple step to do the Bassline Swap Beatmix.

This is the most advanced mix in this book, but it's not such a leap from the Single Phrase Beatmix. It relies on the fact that the types of music I just mentioned tend to follow a formula, and part of that formula is: drums start, followed by drums plus bassline, followed soon enough by all the rest of the stuff (vocals, breakdowns, drops, and so on). Likewise, such tunes usually end with the reverse happening; elements are removed from the production until there are just drums and a bassline left, with eventually even the bassline disappearing, leaving a phrase or two of drums alone to end the track.

If you were to beatmix two such tunes at a typical point (i.e. near the end of the first one and near the beginning of the second one), chances are that one of two things would happen. Either the basslines would clash for a while, because you've overlaid the tunes at a point where the bassline hasn't disappeared from the old tune before the bassline arrived in the new one, or they would be too spread apart, meaning the bassline would end on the outgoing tune while there was still just a drum intro playing on the incoming tune, with the bassline maybe a phrase or more away from appearing. The former could sound bad (especially if the tunes aren't in the same or a compatible musical key), the latter tedious as there'd be a phrase or more of your beatmix with nothing but two sets of drums playing together.

The Bassline Swap fixes this, and puts control back into your hands so you're not relying on those elements lining up correctly, or having to wait until the end of every tune to mix in the next one if you don't want to. This technique lets you try more daring mixes while keeping them tight and sounding good.

How to do it

This is the Single Phrase Beatmix, with some key differences:

1. Make the mix longer. You can do the Bassline Swap Beatmix over a single phrase as outlined above, but as it tends to sound tighter and better than the alternatives, you will sometimes want to have those two tunes playing together for more than a single musical phrase. So start your second tune earlier, and make sure there's plenty of the outgoing tune left so it doesn't run out as you're performing this. On a five minute tune, you're looking for around sixty to ninety seconds left.

2. Start with the low EQ turned all the way down on the incoming tune. The low, lo, or bass EQ knob (see the next chapter for more on EQ) controls how much of the kick drum and bassline we hear, and turning this all the way down immediately takes the thump and power out of your incoming track, making it sound thin and weedy. Happily, assuming the first minute or so of the track is just drums or drums and bass, it also removes the majority of the musical information contained in the track, meaning there's less chance of that musical information clashing with anything remaining in the outgoing track as it completes.

3. Swap the basslines. At a point in the incoming track when the bassline has arrived, or at the point when you know it does arrive, turn its EQ back to normal (twelve o'clock), while simultaneously turning the low EQ of the outgoing track all the way down. Assuming the bassline is still playing on the outgoing track, this has the effect of swapping the bassline the audience hears from the outgoing track's to the incoming track's. As bass is where most of the power of any dance track is, you're switching the audience's attention firmly from one track to the other, but crucially *at a time in your mix that suits you.*

While I have called this the Bassline Swap Beatmix, many DJs use this technique in all their beatmixing anyway, whether or not they're consciously trying to swap basslines, because having two kick drums pounding away together for extended periods is unnecessary. This method lets you stealthily introduce a new track into the mix, only letting it dominate (by moving its bassline up in the mix while removing the old track's) when you're ready. But it works best when you do as I've described and use it to keep the musical interest going by overlapping more of both tracks and controlling which bassline dominates. It gives you freedom to be more adventurous.

Bonus: watch a video demonstrating this technique at http://djtips.co/transition5

Don't be afraid to experiment

All of the above give you starting points for your own mixing, and the variations you end up liking and preferring will often happen by accident, either by necessity ('I've got to mix this tune in *now* or we're in trouble!'), or by experimentation.

It is not always important, for instance, to have a beatmix running in your headphones before you mix it in to the main mix - modern technology and your growing experience will empower you to start a tune playing with the fader open so the audience hears it from the second it starts. On the Bassline Swap, you could have both bass EQs turned down for a bar, half a phrase, or longer to take all the power out of the whole mix deliberately before slamming in the incoming track's bass on the next downbeat and bringing the energy back up.

Many tunes start or end not with drums, but with a beat-less section - some strings, a synth line, some vocals. Far from making them difficult to mix, these elements actually present an opportunity to the DJ who isn't scared of experimenting, because as long as your phrase timing and tempos are correct, you can have the incoming or outgoing drums-only part of one track laid over this beat-less part of the other track, each part complementing the other. Likewise, you'll quickly find that for beatmixing, having just drums playing on one track, or even both, works better than trying to mix more melodic musical sections together, which will usually confuse the audience and sound messy.

Armed with these five transitions and a pile of music you love, go ahead and practise these mixes until you have done each one at least once or twice to your satisfaction. In the next few chapters, you'll meet some extra features that can make mixing easier for you, and make your DJing more fun overall - and I'll let you in on a huge secret for making sure that when you finally get to show your new skills off in public, everything you do sounds good.

Using Sync, Hot Cues And Loops

Introduction

DJs using records on turntables had none of these things. But since DJ CD players and then digital DJ systems controlled by software have arrived on the scene, so have functions that make DJing easier and more creative, and these stand out as ones which have made a huge difference in the way modern DJs operate. They are simple, clever, and will give you much more control over your DJing than that afforded to somebody just using records.

Better have a closer look at them, then…

Sync

Sync does all the manual beatmixing stuff for you. Press one button, and your beats snap together – and stay that way. Controllerism, finger drumming, four-deck mixing, live remixing, re-editing, cue juggling…these are all new DJing paradigms, skills, and techniques that have either been invented or come to the fore with the advent of digital DJing. Doing them relies heavily on automatic syncing of your tunes.

Gear and software equipped with sync analyses the tracks you load up. Then you tap the sync button and, armed with this analysis, your gear does all the things we already know about beatmixing for you. One, it tempo matches the tunes (getting them to the same speed by adjusting the speed of the new one to match the old one); two, it beatmatches them (lining their beats up); three, it holds those beats together as they play, saving you the need to monitor them closely should they slowly drift apart and need some manual correction.

In most systems, you get to choose how much of the above actually happens when you hit that button, and how. You may be able to have your system match the tempos but leave the beats bit to you. And you may be able to alter whether it attempts to line up just beats or tries to get the bars lined up too, or even whole phrases.

Take the time to understand exactly how your particular variant of sync works and be conscious of how your options are set, not least because it will help you should issues occur. What kind of issues? Well, your DJ software may guess the BPM wrong. A track may have a BPM that alters, which may throw things out of sync. Your system may get the BPM right, but guess where the beats or bars lie incorrectly. In these cases, blindly hitting the sync button will make things worse as your software thinks it's offering you a solution, but it's actually causing a problem.

Luckily there are ways you can fix this stuff. All systems have a tap function, where you can literally tap along to a song's rhythm on a button. The system will work out the BPM of your taps and thus the real speed of the track. And most DJ systems also offer a 'beatgridding' function, too. This lets you check and correct the auto-generated beatgrid of the track, which is a grid of lines imposed over it marking where the beats lie, and also where the bars (and even sometimes whole musical phrases) sit. (This stuff happens when your system analyses each tune as you import your music.) Checking and correcting the beatgrid will practically guarantee that sync can do its job right first time, every time, and so make it an essential part of your track preparation if you use sync extensively. Good beatgridding systems can even cope with the slight variations of tempo that inevitably happen when tracks were played with live drummers (i.e. not drum machines), making it possible to sync funk, disco, and rock tracks previously off-limits for DJs wanting to use sync.

Sync saves time, freeing you up to do other things, and as long as you understand what it's doing for you (and what to do if it gets it wrong), it's a great tool.

Hot cues

Back in the 'Understanding Your Decks' chapter, we learned that as well as the play/pause button on your equipment, every type of DJ deck (except record decks) also has a cue point button for setting a temporary point on the track you can easily return to. Hot cues are the same thing except there are more than one of them and they get remembered, so the next time you load the track up, your hot cues are still there, accessible to you by a set of extra buttons or pads on your equipment.

Because they are permanent, you can use them consistently to mark important places in your tracks, such as the first beat, or the place you always like to start mixing from, or the beginning of a breakdown, or even exact words in a vocal part. You can then get creative by using the hot cue buttons to jump from place to place in a track, effectively remixing it on the fly. Therefore you can use them simply to make it easier for you to DJ by marking important sections in your music, or to get truly creative and make something totally new out of a track through deft playing of the hot cues, a skill referred to as 'cue juggling'.

On your particular DJ system, start by learning how to set these, how to delete them, and how to trigger them, and then try marking at least your favourite start point of each track with a hot cue. You'll quickly find they become invaluable tools in helping you get music on to your decks and ready for mixing faster and more easily.

Loops

Looping refers to making a part of a track play over and over again. It first appeared with DJ CD players as 'manual looping' (you manually set the in and out points of your loop), but then quickly developed into 'auto looping'. This means that - armed with a knowledge of where the beats lie in your track through pre-analysis - your DJ system can let you instantly command a perfect loop of a set length of, say, a beat, or a bar, or four bars of music. Looping lets you bring elements under your control rather than being constrained by the timing of what happens in the tracks.

Being able to loop the intro of a track (before much happens) or the outro (so your track doesn't end too quickly) can be a huge aid to transitioning. It can also be used more creatively, for instance to loop a short piece of a vocal or percussion to add flavour to a DJ mix – especially when you use the sync function to keep your loop tightly in time with your other tracks.

Just be sure not to use this feature too often as it does encourage long, drawn-out transitions where not much happens and thus can lead to boring sets. Instead, try being creative with it. Why not loop a small part of a well-known track, for instance, and play that over the previous track to tease your audience with what's coming next before you're ready to perform the proper mix between the two?

While sync, hot cues and loops help you to arrange your beats cleanly, easily and creatively, whether within each track or while mixing, there is a whole set of other functions that let you colour the actual sounds in your tracks themselves. That's what the next chapter covers.

Adding EQ, Filters And Effects

Introduction

These three things can help you to make an average DJ mix sound good, and a good mix sound great. They let you shape and sculpt the sound your audience hears. They let you control the track that's dominating your mix and decide when it is to take a back seat to something else. They let you tune the overall sound to suit your needs, and add exciting new colours to it.

Let's take a closer look at them.

EQ

Otherwise called 'equalisation', EQ refers to the tone controls on your mixer that we first met in the 'Mixer Basics' chapter and then again in 'Bassline Swap Beatmix' in the previous chapter. Usually you'll have three for each channel of the mixer that allow you to boost or cut the bass, midrange and treble parts of the sound of whatever you have running through that channel (it's always better to cut than to add, though, compensating by raising the overall track volume using the gain control). They will turn from seven o'clock to five o'clock, and their flat setting will be at twelve o'clock where there'll usually be a little click to let you know they're set to neutral.

There are three reasons you'll want to use EQ:

1. To EQ the track. Different tracks sound different to each other, tonally as well as musically. Maybe your track sounds a bit dull (that'll be lack of midrange), or is too boomy when the kick drum starts (too much bass), or sounds a bit bright when it's all going on (meaning there's too much treble). By putting your headphones on and listening to the next track, and comparing it to the currently playing one by switching between the two, you can work out any elements that may need to be adjusted.

2. To EQ the transition. When you're transitioning from one track to the next, EQ can be used to introduce and swap elements of both the incoming track and the outgoing one at points you choose. A classic use in beatmixing is the Bassline Swap Beatmix, which I taught you in the 'Five Basic DJ Transitions' chapter.

3. To EQ the room. Whether you're at home practising in your bedroom, or in a club with its own PA system, you may need to use the EQ to get the whole room sounding right. Ideally you want to avoid this, but it can be inevitable, because if there are no EQ controls after the signal has left your mixer (often the case with home monitor speakers, or PA systems where the amplifiers are out of your reach or only have volume controls), the last chance to change the EQ for the room is at your DJ mixer. So while we want to see EQ controls returning to twelve o'clock every time, maybe you'll find the room sounds best with the bass tailed off a bit or the treble boosted as a rule - in which case your default EQ position on your mixer will be different.

Remember that the presence of people profoundly changes the audio characteristics of rooms, so as a venue fills up, you may find your EQing has to change, too. (People soak up bass, so you'll often need to boost this frequency area.)

The point with EQ is that you have to trust your ears. There is no hallowed setting that you're not allowed to change. If it sounds bad, it is, so use your EQ as your first line of assistance in sorting that out. Don't be scared to EQ creatively, changing tracks so they sound far different to the way they were made if it works for you. The tracks are your tools, and you're free to use them how you like in pursuit of creativity.

Filters

Filters belong with effects ('FX'), but they're so important, I've broken them away from the rest. In fact, so have manufacturers, and nowadays you often find a filter control for each channel of your mixer on the mixing section of your DJ controller, right underneath the EQ controls, away from any other effects that might be included with your gear. If you're using DJ software, filter is always one of the options selectable among the other effects.

Think of a filter as a one knob EQ with added swoop. Like EQ, one knob filter controls have a centre point where they're turned off, and there is normally a little click to let you know. Turn the filter knob to the left, and you progressively introduce a low pass filter which only lets the low frequencies through. Turn it to the right, and you're getting a high pass filter which only lets the high frequencies through.

What differentiates filters from the EQ controls, apart from there only being one knob generally, is that they have a musical resonance - the swoop quality I just mentioned. In short, they sound awesome, and are used an awful lot in recording studios to introduce and remove elements from tracks, particularly in breakdowns and builds. Because the filter is a sound so often used in dance music production, having it at your fingertips when mixing is a powerful thing as people enjoy it, accept it, and won't automatically think it's you doing it.

Use filters to introduce a track over a musical phrase or remove the outgoing track slowly. Try them in combination with the EQ controls (for instance, turning down the bass and treble on an incoming track and using the filter to introduce the midrange elements works well when there's a saxophone riff on the incoming track), or to bring a looped vocal element from nothing to the front of the mix. It's easily the most used effect, so experiment with it, especially when you see chances to complement the use of filters already present in the tracks you're playing.

Effects

We've all seen the laptop DJ, hunched in the corner in some venue or other, throwing effect after effect over his mix, using them as crude tools to get from one track to another, and seemingly randomly triggering them because he's bored between mixes. Like someone trying out every ringtone on their new phone in public, it's not good.

The first thing to remember with effects is that less is more. Anything you do in your DJ sets should complement the tracks you're playing and delight your audience, adding something to the overall experience. Used for their own sake, effects sound naff, and even if they don't, they're not necessary.

That said, they can add a lot if used carefully.

If you're DJing on a club mixer, you'll find the effects down the right-hand side, and you can decide which channel they are assigned to with a selector knob. You can also apply them to the whole mix. If you're using DJ software, you usually get two separate effects engines, again assignable to individual channels or the main mix.

They can be broadly divided into two groups:

1. The sweep effects. These are effects that don't naturally have a rhythmic element. Filter is one (see above); phaser, flanger and other chorus-style effects (where you hear a pleasing mix of variants of the incoming sounds) are others – think the plane taking off effect. White noise effects

that actually add whooshing over the top of the existing music are another type. You can use them all like you'd use filters to add an extra something to melodies, making your track sound bigger.

2. The rhythmic effects. Delay is the king here – the 'echoing into the distance' sound. Echo is similar, although often it has a grainier feel to it as it's based on old-fashioned tape echo effects units where the incoming sound was physically recorded on to tape in order to be reintroduced to the mix. How times have changed. Nowadays it's easy to tie the timing of the echoing sounds into the beats or bars so they occur in time with the music, hence me calling these 'rhythmic' effects. They can sound great on vocals, especially *a cappellas* (vocal tracks with the rest of the music removed).

When you're playing with your effects in your practising, try working out which group the effect you're auditioning belongs to, bearing in mind it is possible to add a cyclical rhythmic element to the sweep effects on many DJ systems. Remember the golden rule: less is more. Also remember to be aware of whether you're complementing what's already in the tracks you're adding effects to, or adding something completely new – and if you're adding something completely new, be extra careful that it actually makes things sound better. If not, don't do it.

You may be forgiven for worrying that while other DJs can make their sets sound great using all of these tools, as soon as you try to use them, they may end up sounding terrible. How do you know if your attempts at mixing actually sound any good?

In the final chapter of this step, I'll show you exactly how.

How To Record And Critique Your Sets

Introduction

The first real club night I DJed at (where I was actually mixing the music as opposed to the countless mobile DJ gigs I'd done up to that point) was in the basement of a hotel in the city centre of Manchester, back in the 1990s. My DJing partner Terry Pointon and I sold tickets to all of our friends, hired the venue, rented the PA, took our own DJ gear down, and set up on a table to the side of the bar. Tucked under that table was my hi-fi cassette deck, with a pile of blank cassettes, wired in to a spare output on the mixer. We had been practising for months, and wanted a recording of the whole night to keep forever.

As the place filled up we were playing music at about half volume, deliberately holding back from the main event, but when we were ready, we upped the volume, hit record, and I mixed in the first tune of my planned set. Having friends who shared a love for the new house music scene all in one place was itself amazing, and finally getting to play the music - loud - that I'd had flying around in my head for months previously was mind-blowing. But being able to show off all the mixing that I'd been practising since buying my turntables was the best bit of all. As with so many important gigs in DJs' lives, it changed me forever.

And the best bit? We'd recorded it all.

Afterwards, via DJing at an impromptu after-party in the Bishop of Salford's back garden (that's a story for another time), we ended up in Terry's living room, two cassette tapes in our hands, ready for a triumphant replaying of our glorious DJ sets from earlier. Settling back in comfy chairs, we slipped the first cassette into his tape deck and hit play.

Luckily we laughed, because otherwise we'd have cried. The cassettes were awful - not the quality of the recording or the tunes, but the DJing. The records skipped, the levels were all over the place, the mixing was at best functional, at worst embarrassing...we went from heroes to zeroes in our own minds in the space of one side of a cassette, and it didn't improve as we played through the rest of the recordings.

How did we not know? How did we miss all the bad stuff when we were actually DJing? Why didn't people tell us, stop dancing, leave the venue and go somewhere better? How had this happened?

That recording taught me so much. Firstly, it taught me that as long as the music is right, people will forgive pretty much anything. But more importantly - like a college essay that comes back to you from your teacher covered in red ink - it gave me a crystal clear checklist of things to work on in my DJing, a roadmap for improvement. And the most valuable lesson it taught me? *You cannot judge your own DJing while you're actually doing it*. The only way to judge your DJing is to record your sets and listen back to them, preferably some time later, because only then will you be hearing them how everyone else heard them.

Hopefully, when you were reading the parts of this book that concerned mixing and transitioning, sometimes you asked, 'But how will I know if my fades sound good, or if I've chosen the right tunes for this technique to work, or if I've lined the beats up properly, or if I've actually managed to get the levels right, or, or...?'

The only way you'll ever know any of this stuff is by recording your DJ sets and listening back.

How to record your DJ sets

In order that you don't let the idea of recording your DJ sets paralyse you, it's important to remember that you're doing it to give yourself the opportunity to listen back to your own DJing, not to aim for perfection. (If you were actually making a real DJ mix for release rather than just recording your set, the process would be very different to hitting record and hoping for the best.)

All DJ software has a record button on it, which will give you a digital file that you can add to iTunes, put on your phone, or play back from your computer directly. There are also apps available for smartphones that record whatever you plug in to the phone. If you would like to use one of these, buy the right lead and plug directly into your DJ controller or mixer rather than use the built in microphone, for obvious sound quality reasons.

However you do it, it's essential to get into the habit of recording your practice sessions so it simply becomes part of how you work as a DJ. Start recording at the beginning of a practice session, stop at the end. It's important that even if you completely mess up (put the wrong tune on, have to try whatever the technique is again, and again...), you leave the recording going and push on to the end. It's like the cameras in a reality TV show - the idea is you forget they're there.

Soon you'll find yourself deferring judgement on the things you try as you learn and practise new skills until you listen to the recording later rather than making your mind up there and then as to whether what you did was any good. This is exactly what we want.

Listening back to your recordings

There are two ways to listen to your recordings. The first is to throw them on while you're doing something else. This will give you an overall sense of so many things: the tunes themselves, the track programming, the general levels (does it keep getting quieter or softer, or have you got it about right?), and so on. The second is when you formally sit down and listen to your work, specifically checking the precision of your loops and cue juggling, how your FX experimentations sounded, and whether that brave bit of scratching you tried sounded good or not.

In truth, you'll find yourself flipping between these modes, especially while listening to your own recordings is still a novelty. You'll find yourself rewinding to hear a particularly good mix again, for instance, or doing the same thing to work out why something you thought was wrong at the time actually sounds good, the latter being the kind of pivotal learning moment that only recording your sets can give you.

It's important to leave some time between recording the mix and listening back to it. In my story above, we'd been out partying after the gig before we actually got home to have a listen. I don't suggest you necessarily do that - maybe just sleeping on it would be a more sensible alternative - but it's this time period that eases you out of DJ mode and into listener mode, which is the key to successful listening.

For a similar reason, generally it's best not to listen back to mixes while at your DJ gear, as the temptation to power up and head back into DJ mode is too strong. However, one time when doing this can be valuable is at the start of a mix session, especially if you're not feeling particularly inspired or you've not had time to listen to the last mix you did. You can make notes, get back in the groove, and then be ready to head into today's practising with a headful of new ideas.

So with your skills rapidly improving and your confidence building, your thoughts will turn naturally to what it's all about: playing in public. The whole next step will help you make the transition from bedroom to booth successfully.

Step Four: Playing Out

By this stage of the process, you're ready to venture into public, and this section shows you how. From booking your first gig to everything you need to remember to take, I'll get you out of the door and into the venue. Once there, I'll show you how to set up, how to behave towards everyone from the doormen to the club manager, and how to deal with the inevitable nerves that come with playing out. Once you're up and running, I'll give you stacks of hard-won advice to make sure you read your crowd correctly and programme an amazing DJ set – whatever type of venue you're playing in.

Why You Need To Play In Public

Introduction

I remember, when I was a teenager, starting my own band. We used to rehearse above a furniture warehouse in an old cotton mill, and it got properly cold in there on winter Tuesday nights. And yet we all showed up, week after week. If it hadn't been for the continuous stream of gigs I'd booked for us and the thought of letting the other four down, I am sure at least one or two of us wouldn't have turned up so religiously, but there we were, learning songs, practising arrangements, writing stuff. I learned a valuable lesson back then that has stuck with me through all my years as a performer.

When it comes to learning to DJ, your biggest enemies are going to be lack of time and lack of focus. You don't feel like you can make enough time to learn properly, and when you do make that time, you're really not sure how to spend it, so you start to doubt that you're getting any better. And while you're trying your hardest to collect the music, and master the gear, and work on your techniques, the path to improving just seems to disappear sometimes and there's nothing to guide you through the fog.

However, the lesson of my story above is clear: to make sure you put the work in, you need a goal, and you need that goal to be public. It helps if there's a real risk that you're going to make a fool of yourself if you don't do the work.

Luckily with DJing, there's a simple goal every DJ can set, and it works every time.

Book yourself a DJ gig. Now.

Maybe the reason you're reading this book is because you're bold and you've already done that, but you're scared of messing up. If so, great! You're in the right place. But just as likely, you're already grasping for excuses as to why this isn't the right advice for you. I know this because I've heard all the excuses all before. So you aren't ready? You live too far from a decent venue? Nobody will come? You don't know who to ask? Nobody in your town likes your music? You live in a big city and there's too much competition? Your gear isn't up to it? You haven't got enough kit? Yeah, yeah, yeah.

I have taught thousands of beginners - people who felt like you may do now. And you know what? They always thank me for forcing them to book themselves a gig. You are no different. DJing itself is what demands this outcome. When you signed up for this hobby, you signed up for performing in front of an audience, and the reason you're resisting now is probably because it's getting real. The likelihood is, all I'm doing is reminding you of something you already know.

The truth is that once you've booked yourself a DJ gig somewhere and told your friends and family, the whole dynamic changes. No longer do you fail to turn up for practise sessions. No longer do you find yourself struggling to work out what to do, or getting disillusioned when you start trying to do it. No longer do you worry that you're not getting any better. Instead, you have an all-too-real mental image of the venue, the crowd, you, and what will be going on. And every fibre of your being will be guiding you towards the only acceptable outcome: to do it without making a fool of yourself up there.

Luckily this is DJing, not some kind of elite sport that only a few hundred people in the world can do. It's something you can learn. It's something any music lover can do. And just like you can only get so far learning to play football on your own with a ball in your backyard, you can only get so far learning to DJ with your gear in your bedroom. It's a team sport. You need your crowd.

You want to know something else? The most valuable learning happens in public. That's where you learn to spot what people want. That's where you learn what to do at the beginning, middle and end of the night. That's where you learn how to handle yourself behind the decks and build the energy of a party. Just like you can't get to know a new city by reading the guidebook, you can't really experience what DJing is all about until you play a gig. Then it all makes sense; you get to join the club. That's where you fall in love with it.

That's when other people will call you a DJ.

The final step of this process is about all the things to do to ensure you turn this first gig into a lifetime of great DJing experiences, but it all starts with you dipping your foot into the water. Your first gig doesn't have to be on a festival stage; a party for friends at the little bar on the corner that you love will do. Use your imagination, get something in the diary, and invite everyone you know. The rest of this step will help you to do a great job of it.

How To Pack The Perfect DJ Set

Introduction

One of the great things about my job running the world's biggest online DJ school is when people get in touch with me to tell me how much I've helped them. One person who comes to mind here is David Dunne.

David is a DJ/producer and radio presenter who's DJed all over the world for Ministry of Sound, and who also worked as head of music for MTV UK. He's an old friend who actually gave me my first break in radio, guest DJing on his Kiss radio show back in the 1990s. And he spoke to me because I'd just fixed an issue that had been plaguing him ever since he switched to digital DJing.

'Your advice about how a DJ should only take exactly twice the music they need with them to gigs changed everything for me!' he told me. 'It's so obvious, but I hadn't been doing it since switching to digital, and that one simple change put me back in charge of my DJ sets. I can't believe I forgot that.'

David believes in my idea so strongly he physically copies the tracks he's decided to take with him to his DJ laptop for every gig, and removes all other music. I don't actually recommend you do this (unless you're truly old school like David is), but I do recommend you 'pack a crate' which you will play from at each and every DJ gig in preference to your master collection.

THE PLAYLIST PYRAMID

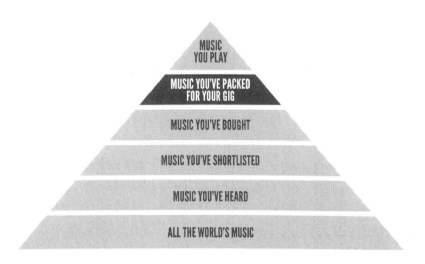

Packing a crate is the fifth tier of the Playlist Pyramid, and one of the biggest secrets of smooth, seemingly effortless DJing once you get to your gig.

Why do this?

For the new DJ, the idea of leaving behind most of the digital music he or she has spent months collecting can sound crazy. Yet counter-intuitive though it may seem, carefully packing a set of possible tunes to play at your DJ gig is an essential step in preparing for it.

When you see a DJ really in the zone - when the tunes are all perfect, the order is amazing, the crowd is loving it, and the DJ seems to *know* what to play next, effortlessly pulling gem after gem from his or her collection - it's because that

DJ has packed a good crate for that event using all the secrets I'm going to give you in this chapter.

Putting it another way: ever seen a DJ with a facial expression somewhere between scared and petrified hunched over a laptop, eyes fixed like a rabbit's in headlights, paralysed, the only thing moving a constant scroll of data entries on their screen? That DJ's panic as they try to find a tune - *any* tune - to play next in their set is precisely what happens if you don't pack a crate for each and every gig.

So here's why it works:

It forces you to think hard about every tune you take. When you're only taking twice the amount of music you need, thinking about what to take and leave behind makes you consider your gig in great detail. You picture the people who you think will come and you're honest about what you think they'll like... and not like. You ask yourself, 'What would I do if...?' and bring a few tunes to cover different eventualities. You learn to respect the hard-working tunes that always seem to work while limiting the number of riskier tunes you pack.

It gets you in the habit of formally preparing for your gig. Establishing a practice session where this is all you do improves your performance once you get to your gig. If you were asked to speak in public you'd run through your speech several times the night before, and in the same way preparing your DJ set gives you the chance to run through your music. This last minute revision has all kinds of benefits, from reducing nerves and raising your confidence to getting you excited about sharing all that great music.

It helps you to perform better. Knowing you've already packed a great set will give you confidence, poise and swagger as a DJ. It'll make you appear to your audience like you not only know exactly what to play next, but you know it with very little effort, having the time to dance, laugh and lead the party, too. That's the kind of DJ people get behind; the kind of DJ who makes great parties happen. And it's largely down to packing a great selection of tunes to bring with you in the first place.

How to know what to take

In David's case, once he had remembered this fact, with all of his experience the old skill of packing the perfect record box kicked back in and he was away. But for the new DJ, especially in the digital age when this skill is optional, some assistance is required.

We've already covered the basic ideas way back in the 'How To Choose And Buy Music' chapter. This is how to build on that work before your gig to make sure you get it right for a particular event.

Start off with the following model, which shows you three distinct sets of views about what music to play on any given DJ night. It frames both what you can and can't do, as well as showing you a sweet spot of tunes that are going to be the stars of your show.

WHAT TO PLAY

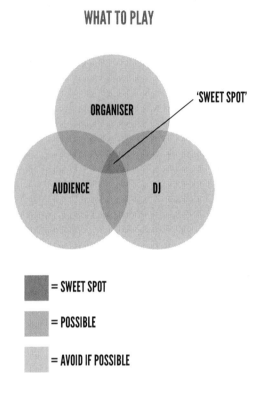

= SWEET SPOT

= POSSIBLE

= AVOID IF POSSIBLE

At the top we have the person who is in charge of the event, whether that is the venue owner, the promoter, or the party organiser. This person will definitely have ideas about the music, ideas that you need to know. If the event is a wedding, you'd better talk to the bride well ahead of time. If it's in a club, there may be music styles the club simply has a blanket ban on because they attract the wrong crowds. If the person in charge is a promoter, he or she may have booked you to play a certain type of music. You need to know this because if you play music you weren't booked to play, no matter how much you and your audience like it, you'll probably get kicked off and maybe sent home without payment.

Next we have your audience. They are a different beast. Just because a father who's booked you for his eighteen-year-old daughter's birthday party doesn't want 'any of that rave nonsense', she and her mates might think differently. Just because the bride and groom give you an exhaustive list of every song they've ever kissed to, it doesn't mean all their friends want to dance to that stuff all night. Within the confines of the absolute dos and don'ts, you've got to consider your audience as a huge priority here. And, of course, you don't know exactly who's going to turn up, but you have to try and work this out. Disregard the audience and only play what is asked of you (or what you like), you'll have empty dancefloors. If you're booked to play at a venue that already has DJs and you don't know the venue or the crowds it attracts, go there and observe - you'll be glad you did.

Finally, you! Great DJs do not play music they don't like. The whole reason you got into this is to be able to play the music you love and feel passionate about, right? So it stands to reason that you need to think of yourself in all of this. Far from being a selfish trait, this is in fact one of the most selfless decisions you can make (it's the 'gas mask' moment - you know the advice on planes: 'Put your own gas mask on before helping other people'). If you're not having fun, nobody else will. Nobody. Else. Will.

'DJing,' one of the DJs from Manchester's legendary Haçienda nightclub, Dave Haslam, told me once, 'is about the transfer of energy from DJ to dancefloor. And I've seen many DJs where the dominant emotion they're transferring is boredom.' Luckily I've taught you to work with music you love, but at this set packing stage, you need to double check that's true about each tune you admit to your set list for the night.

As you're packing your DJ set, you need to be asking three questions about every single track: Is it what's expected? Do I think the audience will like it? Do I want to play this in public myself? The more tracks you can say yes to all three questions about, the better. If you say no to any, at least be aware of that.

Here are some reasons for no answers that could lead to you taking the track anyway:

'It's brand new, but I know it's going to be a big hit and I want to play it. I'll make the audience love it!'

'I know I'm not meant to be playing drum & bass, but it's a big remix of a huge hit…maybe I'll play it at the very end when everyone's happy with what I've done.'

'OK, it's a huge song. I'm not sure if I like it, but I'll give it a go. Maybe seeing the audience reaction will make my mind up for me about it.'

Five steps for packing a great set

I was once called back off holiday at the last minute to play a special DJ set to cover for a very sick colleague. It wasn't any old DJ set, but a sold-out 'classics revival' night, playing underground house music from the late 80s and early 90s, and I was the only person in our circle who had the tunes people were expecting. That said, I hadn't played that kind of set for months. I had done no preparation, and not packed a single tune.

Rushing home, I threw piles and piles of vinyl into bags and boxes, and flew out of the door to the venue. Once I got there, I sat on the dancefloor, my girlfriend handing me records as I flicked through them one by one, deciding if I wanted each for the night or not. The tunes that I wanted, I arranged in piles in a semi-circle around me - little mini-sets of warm-up tunes, floor fillers, diversions into popular genres from the time, someday/maybe tunes, and so on.

I cut it so close to the wire that people were actually walking into the club as I was finishing and there was no music on at all! Yet I still did the preparation, knowing how important packing a crate is to playing a decent DJ set. And the planning paid off. From me being thoroughly annoyed at having my weekend off spoiled, that gig turned out to be one of the most memorable of my life.

I managed to pull that gig off with far-from-ideal set planning through years of experience, but you can do it too if you follow the guidelines I give you here before each and every gig:

1. Pack twice as much music as you need. Say you're planning on playing in a local bar for three hours. You're a pop DJ, and you guess the average length of each song you want to play is three minutes. That means about twenty songs an hour. So you'll probably end up playing sixty songs in your set. Therefore, the crate you pack should contain 120 songs. Why? Because any fewer, and you run the risk of playing a fixed playlist and running out of options for reacting to what the crowd is or isn't enjoying. Any more, and you'll likely be blinded by choice and get analysis paralysis. (Having *more* to choose from actually makes the task *harder*. Think of extensive restaurant menus.)

2. Pack in sequences. Part of being a DJ is the joy of working out what tracks follow each other. It is not really anything to do with the way you transition or mix between those songs, rather it's the fact that they just go well together. As you become more experienced as a DJ, you'll learn by trial and error what does and doesn't go with what, but even at the start of your hobby or career, you'll have a few ideas. Indeed some DJs swear by organising *all* of their music in twos, which if you think about it halves the job of knowing what to play next. I prefer looser mini sets of two, three or four songs that tend to find each other in my collection. Keep in mind the idea of clustering your songs together, though.

3. Visualise your DJ set as you do it. Picture yourself standing behind your decks wherever it is you'll be DJing, and picture the people in front of you near the start of your DJ set. How loud is the music? How busy is the venue? How interested is the crowd? Are people dancing, or relaxing at the bar/seating area? How is this going to change as the night moves on? Asking these types of questions will help you to judge ahead of time the music that may or may not work. It will also give you something to compare your thinking with *after* the gig to see if you imagined right or not. Next time you're packing a set, you'll have learned from that, and your ability to picture your audience will improve.

4. Pick your extra tunes wisely. As you're going to be packing twice the amount of music you will need, you're going to be aware that you'll end up playing only half of the tunes you pack for your gig. But don't fall into the trap of padding out the tunes you really want to play with any old stuff. No DJ *ever* sticks to his or her set-list (unless you're playing a short choreographed festival DJ set, complete with pyrotechnics and visual, and frankly if you were, it'd probably be pre-recorded anyway).

No DJ can pre-guess the makeup or mood of their audience entirely. What you want to play to them may not work. So you will at some point in your set need a plan B, or several plan Bs. By ensuring that as well as taking all the stuff you'd *like* to play, you also take the same number of tunes again to offer you alternatives should Plan A not work out, you'll get all the benefits of the discipline of set-planning while insuring yourself against misjudging your audience. And a strange thing about DJing from a finite number of tunes is that you tend to find the stuff you couldn't get away with earlier in your set often works well later on.

5. Arrange your set in some kind of order as soon as you've chosen the tunes. Of course it makes sense to keep your mini-sequences or pairs together, but packing all of your night's tunes into a rough order takes some of the strain off you when you are ready to perform. DJs traditionally packed from the front to back of their record boxes, with warm-up tunes at the front of the crate, and the set developing further back. With digital playlists, you drag the tunes into a rough order with the front of your crate being the top of your playlist. Most software lets you return to this order even if later on you rearrange the list by genre, BPM or whatever.

This needn't be hugely complicated once you get into the habit. After you've played a few DJ sets, a great way of packing a crate is to look back at your last few gigs and see what worked and what didn't. You can then borrow whole chunks of your DJ crates from gig to gig. (Remember, this is a crate, deciding what music to take. It isn't carbon copying what you do every time.) You'd then typically throw in a handful of new tracks you really want to play, and balance that with some safer stuff you know you can fall back on. As you get more experienced as a DJ, set planning can be that simple – but all great DJs still make time to do it.

Of course, music isn't the only thing you'll be taking with you to your gig. Let's find out in the next chapter what else to pack.

Things To Take With You

Introduction

Packing your bag for a DJ set is a little like packing your bag for a business trip or holiday. Despite all your planning, you will almost definitely find yourself pausing momentarily at the door and running through a mental checklist ('wallet, tickets, phone...') designed to reassure you that even if you've forgotten everything else, you have the essentials.

When it comes to leaving the house to head off to a DJ gig, what you take with you will depend very much on the type of DJing you're doing and what the venue is expecting from you, but it helps to divide your mental checklist up into 'gear, music, other stuff'.

That's how we'll run through what to take with you in this chapter.

DJ gear

Forgetting an essential piece of DJ gear is embarrassing, and worse, it often means you won't be able to play. I started off my DJ career playing mobile shows where I was expected to provide everything from the lights to the PA system to the table to set it all up on. Years later, I remember turning up at my first club-style gig thinking how amazing it was that everything would be provided for me, only to realise that this didn't go as far as headphones (for hygiene and personal preference reasons, a DJ *always* takes his or her headphones along). Ditto your laptop and laptop stand if your DJing involves playing from a computer – nobody provides computer equipment in DJ booths.

As far as the rest goes, though, the best bet is to visit the venue or at least speak to the manager to check. Most permanent venues where DJs play regularly will already have a DJ set-up: usually a couple of DJ CD players and a mixer, possibly a microphone, and definitely a PA system. Whether or not you decide to take any gear of your own (the DJ controller you're used to playing on, a digital vinyl system, record decks, extra control units) will depend upon how comfortable you are using the venue's gear, the quality of its gear, how long you'll be playing for, and what's expected of you.

Some venue managers dislike DJs bringing controllers with them and expect them to play on the already installed gear (although DVS systems are generally tolerated), others won't even set up their existing gear unless you ask them to. Some have state-of-the art fully networked pro DJ systems where you plug a single music USB stick in and it all comes to life like a flight deck, others may have a couple of battered old CD players and a mixer that hardly works. The manager may tell you they've got record decks, but you turn up to find they're buried under a pile of coats in the corner, minus cartridges and needles.

Of course, if you are heading out as a mobile DJ then you are still expected to bring absolutely everything, and don't even expect there to be a power socket near to where you have to set up. From lights to leads to equipment stands to a nice, neat and professional looking facade to tidy your set-up into once it's all rigged, you're a one-man band. But even if you're of the 'have headphones and USB stick, will travel' flavour of DJ, it's always a good idea to take a few spare leads so you can jump in and save the day if something's not working properly. Various audio cables, a spare USB lead if you're a laptop DJ, and a spare headphones adaptor won't take up much space in your bag, and one day you'll be glad you brought them along.

Always protect your gear on the move. Hard flight cases are the ultimate in protection, although softer backpacks, trolleys and shoulder bags provide enough protection in most cases, and are much easier to carry around or smuggle into cabin luggage with you if you're flying. (If you're going for specialist DJ ones, consider plain packs rather than those that scream, 'Highly valuable DJ gear inside'.)

A separate case for your headphones is a good idea (they don't like being sat on). It's the knobs and faders that nearly always get damaged first on DJ gear, especially in soft cases, so you can buy hard acrylic covers that fit snugly over the faceplates of most modern gear, and they're well worth the small extra spend. (They keep the dust off the gear at home when you're not using it, too.)

Back-up music

The big thing to remember about your music is to bring a back-up music source with you, and have a plan as to how you'll get that music playing if disaster strikes. Whether it's nothing more than a few songs on USB or CD to get you past a laptop crash or a whole spare laptop (a common thing among pro DJs), the point is that you must be able to keep the music going come what may, and that means a back-up music source.

Many DJs have music on their smartphones and a simple lead that lets them plug their phone into a spare channel on the club's mixer, making it simple to hit play on a music or DJ app on their phones, throw up a mixer fader, and keep the party going through a laptop reboot. If you'll be DJing from a laptop, this is probably the simplest fallback because you already have your phone on you, so it's just a case of plugging it in before you start.

Other stuff

Most of this is common sense, but if you read the following list and get just one 'a-ha!' moment, it'll be worth the time spent. So: spare shirt and towel (if you're the type that gets hot and sweaty under the lights); something to eat (hungry DJs are irritable DJs, and a bag of sweets keeps forever); your business cards or other promotional material; a pen and something to write on; sunglasses (if playing a beach set or all the way through to dawn); any medications you take; ID (especially if you're young-looking and playing in a club); and that trio of wallet, tickets and phone that started this chapter. Scribble it all down on a checklist. Pin it to your door. Run through it on the way out. Job done.

Next step: arriving at the venue and setting up. The next chapter will make sure you know exactly what you're doing when you get there.

Setting Up In Public Venues

Introduction

I'm sure you know that horrible feeling when you turn up for your first day at a new job and don't know where to hang your coat or where the bathroom is. You need to ask someone to help you with all kinds of silly things as the day goes on - stuff you'll be taking for granted soon enough, just like everyone else does. Your first DJ gig is going to be a bit like that, except you may not even be sure what questions to ask.

This chapter is designed to help you so you can look like - while you may not have DJed in that particular place before - you certainly know what you're doing.

The first rule of playing in an unfamiliar venue is to visit it ahead of time if you possibly can. Whether it's the bar on the corner of your street, your local church hall, or a full-blown nightclub, the manager will usually be more than happy to let you check out their gear, ask what's required of you, and generally scout around the place a day or two before your actual gig date. Just make sure the manager, or someone who can answer your questions, is actually there on the date and time you choose to do this.

How to set up in a bar or lounge

This is many DJs' first public gig: playing a set in a local bar, lounge or pub. Maybe you've managed to get yourself a week-night slot, you could be lucky enough to have got a weekend evening, or perhaps you've convinced a beach bar owner to let you play a sundowner set. Whatever, the bar gig is a tried and tested stepping stone to bigger things as well as a satisfying end in itself.

Generally, bar gigs are characterised by the venue having its own sound system, which is often simply the system it plays music through all week long. That could be the local radio station, a music video TV channel, or the owner's iTunes or playlists from an online streaming station. Bars often don't have their own DJ gear, or if they do, using it is optional, so it's usually OK to turn up with your controller or other system.

If the bar staff are used to having DJs playing, they'll know where they physically want to put you, and may even have a wall-mounted socket for you to plug your mixer or controller into that feeds back to their amplifiers. Some may have a long lead that you're meant to plug into the back of your gear to get the audio to the venue's amps. Power may be from a socket conveniently by the table they want you to set up on, or again they may have an extension lead they reel out to get sockets near to you.

Don't rely on any of these things, though. Carry your own power extension leads and multi-adapters, and every type of audio cable you can think of, including long ones, of the right type to fit into the back of your DJ controller or mixer. Also, consider how you're going to raise your gear to standing height – stooping over a low table for any length of time will give you backache. (A beer crate with a black sheet thrown over it to make it look neat is a good raiser. Carry that black sheet with you.)

Finally, know ahead of time whether you'll need a monitor speaker, and if so, how you'll plug that in. In bars, often you can set up near to one of the bar speakers, which is fine, but other times this isn't possible. You may end up away from the music, your nearest speaker pointing in the opposite direction to you. DJing without being able to hear your own music properly is not fun and makes beatmixing harder because of the few extra milliseconds it takes for the sound to reach you from a speaker across the other side of the room. Some bar DJs carry a single powered speaker with them to plug into the booth or second master output of their DJ mixer or controller to use for this purpose.

How to set up in a club

Unlike bars, clubs of course have sound systems, lights, and a DJ area as standard. They also usually have their own gear, although this isn't always set up for you (increasingly nowadays venue owners understand DJs often bring at least some gear, so they will have their own stuff set up to your specifications on your arrival). You need to know if you're expected to use their gear or if it's OK to bring your own, which varies venue to venue, and country to country. Clubs generally have a monitor speaker or speakers, though, which will be plugged in and ready to go once you're all wired up.

Once you're clear ahead of time about these things, on arrival your job is to set up any gear you'll be using and plug it into the venue's existing system. If its gear is permanently set up and you're plugging in a DJ controller, you'll be looking for a spare channel on the mixer. Make sure it is turned down before you plug in your stuff for a test.

One of the problems with club gigs nowadays, especially if you're not the only DJ, is everyone has their own gear, which can make DJ booths precarious places at DJ switchover time. The golden rules are to talk to the DJ you're taking over from, although no more than necessary, and try to get around the back of the club mixer to plug in as efficiently and unobtrusively as you can no more than ten minutes before the end of the previous DJ's set. Digital vinyl systems present a particular problem because you often need to unplug the venue's CD players or record decks to plug your DVS box in, so again, being courteous, considerate and communicative is important.

Better venues have a sound technician on hand to help with all of this stuff, which is a godsend because that person will know everything inside out. In that case, your job is simply to find them and do exactly what they say. They will expect you to let them do the setting up, so don't try and do any of it yourself. Conversely, often there's nobody at a venue when you arrive who knows anything at all about setting up the DJ, so you may be scouting around for where to turn absolutely everything on yourself if you're not careful. Again, knowing this in advance is invaluable, so do visit ahead of time if you can.

How to set up as a mobile DJ

Unlike either of the above scenarios, as a mobile DJ, you are expected to bring absolutely everything you need with you. If DJing in a bar is like a night away in a basic hotel, and a club gigs is like staying in a four or five star hotel, mobile DJing is like wild camping. If you haven't brought what you need along, or you don't know how to set it all up yourself, you're probably going to have to live without it.

One thing that most venues have is power, but let's assume you're playing somewhere where you can't plug in. As you're carrying your own DJ gear, amplifiers, speakers and lights, you'll need enough cables and sockets to get all of this plugged in, but don't assume there will be a socket near to you, so take heavy duty extension cables that can handle the power requirements of your amps at full swing. Make sure you uncoil them fully even if you don't need their full length (not doing so can cause them to get hot and even trip out when you turn the volume up).

Remember to bring a DJ table or equipment stand, a facade to hide your cables and connectors once set up, heavy duty tape to secure any cables you need to run across the floor, and stands for your PA speakers to get them to audience head height (and any safety attachments to stop them toppling over). Many occasional mobile DJs hire this stuff gig-by-gig rather than owning it. If you choose to do so, make sure you set it all up and see it working at the hire company, and ask any questions about it all there. Even better, hire from a company who will bring and set it up at the venue for you and take it away afterwards.

Unlike with bar and club DJing, where someone else has got the evening's entertainment covered to a varying degree (there's always another DJ hanging around if you mess up, or the staff can stick a CD on), mobile DJs can make or break the whole event, and the amount of equipment you need to bring adds extra responsibility to you personally. All of this makes mobile DJing harder to wing. If you want to do this type of DJing seriously, definitely enquire about and get the right performance licence for your country to let you play venues where there's no public music licence, and also ensure you have bought proper public liability and insurance cover. Many countries have at least one mobile DJ association that can help you with this, and much more.

How To Behave At A Gig

Introduction

Fatboy Slim got it right when he said, 'A good DJ is always looking at the crowd, seeing what they're like, seeing whether it's working, communicating with them. Smiling at them. And a bad DJ is looking down at what they're doing all the time and just doing their thing that they practised in their bedroom.'

In this book I've given you tips to be confident and perform solid, simple DJ mixes (so you're not doing the 'what I practised in my room' bit too much) from a tightly chosen set of tunes (saving you looking down at your laptop all the time, panicking about what to play next). Don't underestimate how these two tactics can alter how successful you are when you are actually playing.

But whether you succeed at any given DJ gig is affected by the way you behave long before you play your first tune. In order to do a great job of DJing, you need to have the management, staff and whoever booked you on your side, no matter how nervous or out of your depth you might be feeling. (There's a whole chapter on dealing with DJ nerves after this one.) And doing so requires you to understand properly where you fit in with everyone else on the night.

What managers really want from DJs

A venue manager has a hard job. From managing his or her staff (many of whom will be on part-time or casual contracts and probably inexperienced) to dealing with stocking the drinks, to liaising with the door people, to handling the promoters or venue hirers, to taking responsibility for all the money coming over the bar, to ultimately being responsible for the happiness (and behaviour) of everyone in the venue, he or she has a lot to juggle. What they have zero time to do is worry about the music – at least, not in any sense that you or I would worry about the music. It doesn't matter if that manager is the biggest music fan in the world, someone who may adore DJing and lives for music, on any given night working in their venue, they will probably notice what you're doing a total of two times: once to say, 'OK, music's on, good' and a couple of hours later to check it's going OK. ('Dancefloor busy or getting there? Can I see a few smiles? Excellent. Now, on to…')

So even if you've been diligent and checked the place out ahead of time, maybe even had a conversation about the music with the manager, on the night is not the time to do that unless they approach you to do so. If they do, listen and do what they say. Apart from that, do what you've been booked for. What the manager wants from you is to be reliable and professional. That's it. Save the music chat, and understand you're a small part of a much bigger machine.

How to get everyone else on your side

The bar staff, doormen, greeters and anyone else working at the venue the night you're playing are your hidden army. They can make your night fun, or make you feel like you're fighting an uphill battle. They are the people who will subtly help you to set the mood and tone for your crowd. Get them on your side, and your job is going to be much easier.

Here are some simple tips for doing just that – well, I say they're simple, but the number of DJs who don't do this stuff always baffles me:

Turn up on time. No DJ, no party. Footballers don't turn up late for games. Applicants don't turn up late for job interviews. You must never turn up anything other than bang on time for a DJ gig. The first person who will notice is the manager. Then everyone else will too. Not good.

Turn up alone. You have been hired to do a job. Not you and your posse of mates, or you and your girlfriend or boyfriend. You. Don't ask for a free guest list, and don't make the first impression any staff member has of you that of someone trying to herd a load of people unannounced into the venue. This is not OK. Turn up alone, and if you've pre-arranged for your posse to attend or been given an invited guest list, make sure they don't all arrive with you.

Be presentable. Don't throw any surprises with your appearance or hygiene. Arrive clean and tidy. You don't need to be in a dinner jacket just because you're playing a formal event (you're the DJ, not one of the guests, although it doesn't hurt to check), but whether it's a cool club night, a street party, or your sister's school prom, you need to give the impression that you're professional and reliable.

Be sober. When the now world-famous Haçienda nightclub in my home town of Manchester was on the up, it was looking for a new resident DJ. Good things were being said about the resident of a rival club across town, so the manager decided to give him a go. Unfortunately, he turned up late and blind drunk. Needless to say, he didn't get the job. A few months later, the fame of the place had risen to such heights that its DJs were invited to tour the USA and play amazing venues across the country, an experience that launched their careers into new waters. Yet this guy missed out, big time. So don't be like him. Don't turn up drunk. It never makes you a better DJ, whatever you might tell yourself.

Be professional. Have you heard of the 7Ps, as used by the British Army and US Marine Corps? They go like this: 'Proper Planning and Practice Prevents Piss Poor Performance'. Really, this whole book until this point has been designed to get you to this stage. Luckily, you're more ready than you think. You know the answers to most of the silly questions amateurs would ask. That said, if you're not sure about something, don't plough on - do ask! That's what professionals do too.

Be friendly. Shake hands. Smile. Look people in the eye. Ask names. Remember those names. Strike up conversations with the staff. Be easy to be around. Don't discriminate – the bathroom attendant is one of the most important people to have onside at a gig (you definitely need priority there when nature calls in the middle of your set). Bar staff who you befriend when the venue is being set up will pass a drink to you over the heads of a six-deep crowd at the bar later on as you nip away from your gear, parched. Doormen you can call by name will help you deal with sticky situations with drunken customers should you ever need them.

Set the tone

The overriding mission you have here is to set the tone, and do so early. Simply being nice will get all the important people on your side; the good vibes at any event spread out from the DJ, and you've just recruited yourself a small army of helpers. The bar staff will give you a thumbs up when you're doing well, feeding back into your confidence. Get one or two of your new friends dancing behind the bar a bit and it will spread to your crowd, encouraging them to buy a second drink and settle in for the night. Smile and be friendly from the off before anyone is even in the venue, and you'll naturally segue into continuing to do so as your dancefloor is filling.

You'll be, to paraphrase Fatboy Slim from our intro, looking up, seeing what's going on, smiling. You'll be spreading the vibe. DJing, as we know, is about transfer of energy, and your attitude and demeanour from the off is where it starts. Get your DJ behaviour right, and you're ready to play a great DJ set in public, perhaps for the first time. Little things you do early on grow into bigger things later, like carefully tending the first flame of a fire that will eventually keep you warm for the whole night.

There's just one slight issue that appears to affect every DJ I've ever known, myself included. Let's get it dealt with…

Nerves And Confidence

Introduction

The very first time I got to DJ in a bar I'd wanted to play right at the start of my DJ career, I spent weeks practising. Indeed, I was so worried that I prepared the whole set, and had it all written out on a small card that I hid under the DJ booth to consult, mix by mix, throughout - even though my hands were shaking so much I could hardly hold it.

Not long afterwards, my first club gig saw me being sick in a bin outside the back door, again through sheer nerves. A few years later when I was well and truly established as a DJ, I was playing at 5am at Privilege in Ibiza in the main room in front of thousands. I had to walk a gang plank across the swimming pool (yes, there is a swimming pool inside the club) to get to the DJ booth, which was situated right in the middle of it. When I got there at 10pm, I was so consumed by nervousness that I used my VIP pass to find somewhere nobody I knew could possibly find me and hid for seven hours, talking to nobody, feeling ill to the core, missing all the fun.

Oh yes, I understand DJ nerves. This chapter shares what I've learned over the years about performance anxiety so you can hopefully deal with it and move on to play a great DJ set.

Why we get nervous

People forget that DJing is performing, it's being up on stage. It's slipping into character, just like singers and actors do. They are allowed to be nervous before a performance, and so are you. In fact, it would be strange if you didn't get nervous before a gig. After all, you're quite likely in an unfamiliar place, you've considered in graphic detail what could go wrong, and you're thoroughly scared about making the switch from the private you to the public you – the version of you that is about to have a great time, play amazing music and bring a roomful of adoring people along for the ride. In the quiet before the storm, those imminent good times feel so impossible an outcome that your irrational mind decides they're simply not going to happen. Self-doubt creeps in. You start asking yourself what the hell you're doing there at all.

But the thing is, all of this is perfectly normal, and it's because you care – pure and simple. If you didn't care, you wouldn't feel any of this because you wouldn't be invested in the outcome. Once you've reminded yourself of this, it's simply a case of dealing with the feelings. Luckily, there are things we can do.

Conquering DJ nerves

There are three tactics I use when I get nervous, and in my experience of coaching DJs, they help a lot to get you out the other side of the often unavoidable pre-gig nerves.

1. Remember that nobody can see your nerves. The chapter before this one gives you the blueprint for what outward impression to give to everyone else. Remember what's going on inside doesn't show on the outside if you don't let it.

My girlfriend - now wife - used to come into the DJ booth when I was in my first hour of warming up a club night I used to promote and DJ at. I'd be smiling away, dancing a bit, shaking hands as people arrived, giving friends a nod and a thumbs up. She'd be having a great time herself, wanting to share in mine.

Making sure the crowd couldn't see me, I'd often then turn to her and growl, 'I'm playing awfully. There's nobody here. It's going to be a disaster. How many times do I have to remind you I'm working? Can't you leave me alone?'

Nerves. I wanted her to understand because I didn't want to fake it in front of her, but she still week after week found it hard to believe I was feeling like that on the inside compared to the impression I was giving everyone else on the outside. You have to remember that some of your crowd might be feeling nervous too, simply about their night out. Your job is to lead from the front, and be strong. This is one time where faking it until you make it is absolutely the right thing to do.

2. Have a well-rehearsed plan B. By the time you get to play your DJ gig, you'll have at some point considered everything from nobody dancing (I still have this as a recurring dream, by the way, three decades into my DJing career) to the music suddenly cutting out (ditto), and all the other things that might possibly go wrong. The trick is to face head-on all of these fears, ask yourself, 'What's the worst that could happen?' then decide how you'd behave and get out the other side. Having a selection of guaranteed floor-filler tracks in your library to use if all else fails can calm your nerves. Having a rehearsed plan B should your laptop crash or USB drive fail will help you put that worry from your mind. Work through your 'what if' list, and remember that DJing isn't brain surgery or flying a passenger jet – nobody gets killed if you don't perform at your best.

3. Remember it's going to pass. Sometimes in life, even though we know the outcome of something, we can't change how we feel through the process. I run marathons and have done for years, and regularly put in thirty or more miles of training a week. You'd think I'd have that one all worked out, right? Yet often when I start off on a training run early on a cold morning, my muscles aching from the last time, I find my brain telling me, 'What are you doing? You're not going to get around this circuit. Stop, you can't do this…' It never gets any better. Yet ninety minutes later, pulling up outside my door feeling great, I realise that the horrible feeling lasted just a few minutes right at the start.

It's the same with DJing – only DJing doesn't hurt so much. I actually believe it's impossible to stay in that highly stressful mental state for too long, and simply pushing on with what you've got to do is all that's needed to come through it. With DJing, it might take twenty minutes or it might take an hour, but sooner or later, you'll relax and realise you've been having fun for a while now. Job done! You're out the other side. Have faith, because this always happens.

'It's not all about you, petal...'

A good friend of mine and a great DJ, Dan Bewick, once gave a talk at one of our DJ seminars about how to be a warm-up DJ, and that was one of his pieces of advice. Really, the last two chapters have been all about this: realising that as the DJ, your job is a great one, but there's a lot more going on at any venue - some of which you can influence, some of which you can't. The best you can do is constantly remind yourself of that and play your part as well as you possibly can.

If it's practical to do so, occasionally leave the DJ booth and spend a bit of time with the audience, seeing the night from their point of view. Early on in the night, walk around the dancefloor checking the speakers sound OK. As the venue is filling up, go and get a drink and have a little smile with the bar staff. As your dancefloor starts to move, make an excuse to pop out quickly and greet somebody you know out there. Not sure what direction to take the night in once you've got everyone dancing? Put a long track on, head out to the floor and ask yourself, 'What would I want to hear next if I was here on a night out?'

Of course, this isn't always possible (there's no way I was walking back across that gang plank once I'd got to the DJ booth over the swimming pool in the Ibiza club), but do it if you can. Ultimately, it'll remind you that 'it's not all about you, petal'. You'll be a better and less nervous DJ as a result.

So we've reached the stage where you're ready to start playing your first DJ set in public. You've done all the preparation and started playing your DJ set. This is what DJing really comes down to: you, a crowd of people, and a pile of music. So how do you know exactly what to play next, and after that, and after that?

That's what the next chapter is about.

How To Programme A DJ Set

Introduction

DJ sets come in all shapes and sizes. They are as varied as the venues, crowds, equipment, music, and events where people dance to pre-recorded music. They can be planned or impromptu, performed or pre-programmed. They can be for a handful of people or a festival crowd of tens of thousands. And, as we know, they can be played on everything from a smartphone to a pro DJ set-up.

But the chances are that wherever in the world you're reading this right now, nearby someone will be stepping up this evening to play music that people will end up dancing to, and – despite the amazing variety of DJ gigs out there – the large majority share a lot more in common than differences. Music gets played. People dance to it. Hopefully someone gets paid for that, and this chapter and the next one are about exactly what to do when that person is you.

As you've practised many times to get to this point, the only difference between this type of DJing and that which you're used to is that, finally, you're doing it in front of other people. This is scary and exciting…and it's also the whole point of DJing. Ultimately, it's not about BPM, or phrasing, or anything else. When it comes down to the final judgement, DJing is really about one thing only: what you play next.

THE PLAYLIST PYRAMID

What you actually end up playing in any given DJ set is the pinnacle of the Playlist Pyramid, the only part anyone else sees. But it's all the work that's gone on beneath it that makes it all seem so effortless to your audience.

Knowing what to play next is a lifetime's work, and it's work that's never done. Even if you're one of those people who thinks about their DJing all the time - and you most definitely should be if you want to become truly good at it - it's a question you'll never find all the answers to. You'll smile to yourself, remembering times you knew a song would work, and it did. You'll look for reasons why something worked really well when you didn't expect it to. You'll try to decipher why a certain tune that smashed it one week fell flat on its face the next. You will - and I promise you this is true - come up with great mixes in your dreams, mixes that you'll simply have to try out on waking up. But you'll also replay over and over as you try to fall asleep the times you thought you had a winner to play next only to clear the dancefloor with it.

So if the above has put the fear into you, it's time for me to pull you back from the brink and share some tactics that'll stop you freezing every time you need to make this decision - which, let's face it, is going to be every three to six minutes throughout your DJing career.

The good news is that you are already set up to make great choices about what to play next (you've practised lots, and you've actually packed a set for your gig beforehand), and so from this point, you can do a decent job simply by remembering the seven guidelines that follow. At the end of this chapter I'll share some pitfalls to avoid which will give you confidence that even though music selection is the most important part of DJing, to be ignored or taken for granted absolutely at your peril, it is something you are perfectly capable of mastering.

Seven ideas for choosing the perfect next track

1. Play the song instinct is telling you is right. You've done an awful lot of practising. You've recorded countless mixtapes. You've listened back to your efforts plenty of times away from the decks through the ears of a listener. And with the work we've done on simple, clean transitions, you know that you're capable of successfully mixing it in, one way or another. So yes, that song in your head is probably the right song to play next.

2. Pick something in a similar BPM, genre or key. In order to carry on the vibe you've created, use the power of digital sorting to arrange or filter your set list by BPM, genre or key quickly and pick something similar to what's currently playing. Try doing all three – look at only your house music, sort it by BPM, then choose a track in the same or a compatible musical key (you may have to enable the column that displays musical key in your software or on your equipment, and read up in your manual about the exact system your set-up uses for analysing and displaying songs in compatible musical key to you). Now you'll have a song that stands a good chance of carrying on the vibe and that you stand a good chance of being able to transition to easily.

3. Pick something totally different in tempo, genre or key. Sometimes, the exact opposite of the above is what's required (i.e. a change of BPM, key or genre), but playing randomly without thought is very different to doing so for a reason. Maybe you've been playing as per the point above for a few songs and the energy level is now flagging a little. This is one circumstance where a change of tactic can work really well for you. The point is to be aware of how you've been playing in order to have a sense of whether such a change might be appropriate.

4. Pick something that's worked before. Let's not overcomplicate things or make them harder than they have to be here. If you've got a song that's worked well for you before in front of an audience, either when played immediately after the currently playing song or generally, it's got a much higher chance of working well again for you. There's nothing wrong with playing the tunes you know, your audience knows, and everyone likes, over and over. While you're rarely going to want to play the same tune twice in the same night, you can expect to play your most popular songs countless times over the weeks, months and years.

Hint: any 'History' section in your DJ software is a great place to look back and remember what's worked for you previously.

5. Play something you've never played before. In direct opposition to the above, at times you are absolutely going to have to take the risk and drop into something nobody knows. Today's new tracks are tomorrow's hits, and part of the job of the DJ is to educate as well as entertain. After all, you are hearing more music sooner than most of your audience, so it's only natural that you're going to pick up on great new tracks a bit earlier than the majority of them will. Have the balls to play them! A good tip here, though, is to know what you're going to play next before doing so, just in case the new song doesn't work and you want to move smoothly into something else a little quicker than you'd planned.

6. Pick something that lyrically matches the moment. This is one area where DJs will always win out over automated playlists or jukeboxes. It could be playing songs that refer to the current weather, or contain the name of the town or venue where you're playing, or have lyrics that encourage people to dance, or reflect the current mood in your town or city (songs about togetherness after bad events; songs about being champions after your big local sports team wins something). We all know songs where the lyrics really reflect how we feel, right? What songs do you have that can do this for a whole venue?

7. Play a hit. I've left the most obvious till last, but big tunes everyone knows generally fill dancefloors, and to a lesser or greater extent every DJ is expected to do some of this. You don't automatically have to go Top 40 here; a classic tune that fits the moment may be exactly the right thing to play, or a big new song that everyone knows from a current film or commercial may work, too.

Five programming pitfalls to avoid

DJs who make it past their first few gigs have an unwritten code of survival beaten into them by the journey. While the tips above contain plenty of ideas to help you develop your ability to find great tune after great tune effortlessly, what follows is a list of rookie mistakes to avoid. Some of them may seem reasonable, possibly advisable, and even those that you can see are wrong you can probably sympathise with, but they're wrong, nonetheless. Do the above and avoid doing the below, and you're 80% of the way there.

1. Don't start every tune search in your master collection. Want that classic laptop DJ look: hunched over your laptop, eyes frightened and staring as you browse through hundreds and hundreds of tunes, unable to pick the next one through analysis paralysis? Simple – play your sets from your master tunes list. Otherwise, it's a complete no-no. Much better to do what I suggest (and what many new-to-digital DJs learn the hard way), which is to pack a crate of music carefully before your gig and play from that. Less is more. The restriction will force you to prepare well beforehand and make your sets sound better on the night – plus it will take an awful lot of the strain off your shoulders.

2. Don't start the search for each next record with the question: 'What do I have that will mix with this?' Instead, find the right track to play next and then find a way to transition into it. In this book are several failsafe ways of performing perfectly acceptable, clean and simple transitions that will work with any next track you may have planned. Aim to get track choice after track choice perfect, and let the mixing take care of itself. Or to be harsher, your inability to mix like a seasoned pro just yet shouldn't ever deny your audience the chance to hear the best music for right now, and the only way to develop those ninja mixing skills is by challenging yourself with the correct tracks in the first place.

3. Don't reach the last few seconds of the currently playing track with nothing ready to play next. Bad for obvious reasons, but common, leading to the DJ throwing anything at all on to the other deck and mixing it in poorly to avoid radio silence. The solution is simple: line up the *very first track* that occurs to you as a reasonable choice to play next immediately. Once it's ready, you're then free to go off searching for something better, knowing your back is covered should you end up finding nothing.

4. Don't play every request you're asked for. 'I don't know what I'm doing! It's so cool the audience is requesting stuff! They're really helping me out of a hole here,' said no good DJ, ever. Don't get me wrong, requests are often great (anything that tells you about your audience is valuable), but the best use of requests is to confirm your instincts about what you're planning to play (in which case: 'Nice choice, I'll play it later for you' is the appropriate response) or to remind you of a current style or a big hit you've temporarily forgotten about. The rest – to put it politely – are usually best ignored. Always remember that you are there because you spend more time and money on music than your audience does, you've studied dancefloors and DJs and you know a bit about what goes into a well-structured, well-paced DJ set. You are there because all this has given you style and taste above mere mortals. Don't let inappropriate/frequent/insistent requesters blow your ship off course.

5. Don't panic! Despite your best efforts, sometimes (and probably at least once in any DJ set) things go wrong. You play a tune that clears the dancefloor. You regret the tune you've just put on, even though it doesn't clear the dancefloor. You accidentally load the wrong song (the one next to the one you wanted in the list, usually) and only realise the fact when you mix it in. You play a tune the DJ before you played, only you weren't around then to know that. You build up to a big tune you've been dying to play only to discover you forgot to bring it with you.

There is only one response: move on calmly with a smile. Style out the inevitable few minutes until you can play another great tune and all will be forgotten. It will, trust me. This is DJing, not open heart surgery. Nobody's gonna die. Be cool.

'How do you make a statue of an elephant?' someone asked a sculptor once.

'Easy,' he replied. 'Get the biggest granite block you can find and chip away everything that doesn't look like an elephant.'

Choosing the tracks that will make the perfect DJ set for the people in front of you right now is both as simple and as difficult as that. This chapter has given you some of the tools and guidelines. Your audiences will give you the rest.

But while every audience is different, one thing great DJs have is a finely honed knowledge of the nature of the audience at certain types of gig - rules of thumb that can assist in programming choices. So to end this step, in the next chapter we'll take a detailed look at how to approach programming your sets specifically for three of the most common types of gigs: bars, clubs, and mobile.

How To Play Bar, Club And Mobile Gigs

Introduction

When you DJ in public for the first time, your gig will more than likely fall into one of three types: bar, club, or mobile. The boundaries between these broad areas are often blurred (a bar that turns into a club later on in the night, a private party in a public venue, or a DJ being booked to play a club-style mobile gig for a trendy crowd, and so on), but it's good to consider these three types of event separately. Despite the crossover, they are distinct in many ways - not least the way in which the DJ approaches playing to the crowds. Definitely read all of what follows, whatever type of gig you are to play, because there is valuable stuff for you to learn from any type of DJing, whether or not it's the type you're interested in or end up spending the majority of your DJ career doing.

How to DJ in bars

I DJed in countless bars before I managed to make a living as a club DJ. It's an apprenticeship and an art in itself.

A bar gig will be in a venue where people come to socialise, and they usually don't pay to get in. It could be a trendy lounge, a beach bar, a fun pub, a beer garden - anywhere where someone is playing records to replace the usual background music. It's performing in public, but it hasn't got the intensity of a club gig.

When you're DJing in a bar, it is important to remember that you're setting the mood for the patrons, most of whom probably haven't come specifically to hear your DJ set. You'll be louder than the usual background music, but not massively so, and people will expect to be able to hold a conversation even when you're in full swing. The biggest trick when DJing this type of venue is, in both volume and musical style, to walk this line skilfully: be noticeable, but not overly so. Don't expect huge responses or packed dancefloors; you're looking for smiles, feet tapping, heads nodding. Your job is to add a human element to what would normally be playing in the background at the venue, delivering just enough of something extra that people say, 'Hey, it's good here! Let's buy another round of drinks…'

But as well as the constraints, you have freedom. To start with, you're usually playing the whole night, not just a pre-determined (and often short) time slot as tends to be the case in clubs. You don't have to fill a dancefloor and keep everyone there, which means you can play a broader choice of music. Bar gigs – especially when you're playing to a 'clubbier' crowd, maybe in an urban venue where people move on to clubs later on – are a good place to try out music you wouldn't dare play at peak-time in a packed club, or music you love but that isn't hugely dancefloor-oriented (after all, there is much more *music you can dance to* out there than *dance music*, whatever the latter means for you and your crowds).

Bear in mind when DJing this type of set that your crowd will be drifting in and out of the venue throughout, so there's less of a defined beginning, middle and end. Rather than playing a warm-up section, followed by a peak-time part of your set, followed by some kind of closing sequence where you bring it all together, you'll be playing more cyclically. Let's say you're DJing at a beach bar where you've decided the music is going to be laid-back deep house, funk, reggae and soul. What you're looking for is everyone to get a taste of what you're about, whatever time they turn up and, within reason, for however long they stay (one drink, two drinks, the whole night…). Therefore look to play a bit of everything every twenty to thirty minutes, because otherwise, you run the risk of being thought of as a reggae DJ, or a deep house DJ, or a funk DJ, when really you're a curated blend of all of those things.

Rather than sorting your set list by genre or energy level, then, it is a good idea at bar gigs to look for good transitions using other methods. Sorting your music by BPM is one such way (you can jump around the genres wildly, but if you're keeping stuff at around the same tempo, it'll likely sound like you've thought about it). Another favourite is to sort by key, either within the BPM constraints or outside of them. Again, with simple, functional mixes between tracks that have the same overall vibe but may be in completely different genres, the glue that holds them together could be matching keys.

Finally, bar gigs, more than any other, are about flexibility. The place may quickly fill up for some reason, then be empty half an hour later. You'll have to adjust the volume and content of your set accordingly. You may be called on (often by phone) to start earlier, or the whole thing may be called off at the last minute (beach bars and rain don't mix, for instance). The bar owner may decide to turn on the TVs and pump the commentary from a big sports event around the venue right in the middle of your set, and you have no choice but to wait until afterwards to continue your job (may as well grab a drink and enjoy the game). You may end up with people dancing, or get sent home early from a quiet night.

But if you can make unpredictability and variety your friends, take pride in learning how to create a vibe that rises above automated pumped music, and do it regularly and professionally ('That guy who plays Tuesdays at the bar on the corner is good…'), bar gigs can be both a stepping stone to greater things and an end in themselves.

How to DJ in clubs

For many DJs the first real club gig is a rite of passage – despite the fact that it's very likely to be a warm-up when there's nobody there apart from you and the bar staff. Just the chance to flex your muscles on a big sound system in a real DJ booth is enough to give any self-respecting bedroom DJ goosebumps, and rightly so – in nightclubs, more than anywhere else, people come for the music, and you're expected to get them dancing.

Unlike in a bar or at a mobile DJ event, in a club you're unlikely to be playing the whole night. Some of my best nightclub gigs have been doing just that – playing regularly from 10am to 4pm in front of a home crowd – but it's rare. Usually, you'll be given a slot, and hopefully you can get one of a couple of hours at least, although the one hour or even forty-five minute slot is common (and it's not a new phenomenon, either – rave flyers were stuffed with dozens of names way back in the early 90s when it all began for my peers and me). Frankly there's little you can do in such a short time, but who'd turn it down? So let's look at how to play it.

If you've been given a warm-up slot in a club, your job is to soothe, tease and nudge the dancefloor from empty to being ready to take off. It's harder than playing the main slot, but can be even more satisfying because you see progression. (You can get hooked on warming up, and to this day a decent-length warm-up slot remains my favourite type of DJing.)

Musically, you're looking for slower, melodic, familiar tunes that don't go past mid-energy; this isn't the time for club bangers or end-of-night floor-fillers. You can afford to slip in a few weirder, riskier tracks, but equally you can play old favourites, both of which you may shy away from later on when only the latest cuts or a narrower selection of music is usually necessary to keep the club close to boiling point.

The key to playing a great warm-up, though, is patience. When people arrive at a nightclub, they do not want to dance. They are almost avoiding the issue; there's stuff to do with coats, there are drinks to buy, a new environment to get used to. It's a time to shake off the stresses of the day and relax, and that doesn't happen in five or even thirty minutes. Only later does dancing come on to the agenda. Your job is to gauge that and raise the pace accordingly - too slowly, and you'll bore people; too quickly, and you'll scare them off. If you do accidentally move too fast, rein it back a little for twenty minutes and then slowly raise the pace again. When you do move up a notch, don't go for the full throttle; hold things there for a few songs before another subtle shift upwards. Again, gauge and move back if you're doing too much, too quickly. And keep cool. Keep smiling. Play the longer game. A warm-up takes time.

Luckily, you have one secret weapon that will help you to do this every time: girls.

The truth is, girls like to dance more than boys do. The dancefloor is one of the few places where women's behaviour tends to be less inhibited than men's. Girls don't seem to have the 'I look ridiculous' block that prevents men from expressing themselves this way, at least until everyone else is. Groups of girls dancing together are normal; groups of men aren't. Girls will encourage each other, whereas boys will be more likely to snigger and put each other's efforts down. Men tend to dance to show off to girls; girls just tend to dance. Whatever, the smart DJ - especially the smart warm-up DJ – grasps the fact that appealing to the girls is essential to get things started. If you can get the girls on the dancefloor, the boys will follow.

So how do you do it? You play tracks that appeal to the female half of your audience. Think tracks with vocals, great basslines, and enough familiarity in them to go straight for the feet of females. But more importantly, watch the girls in your venue. If you can get a small group of girls interested, work out what you played that did it, and find a bit more of the same. You'll soon discover the magic tracks that appeal to your female audience, and they'll become your friends. Ex-Haçienda DJ Dave Haslam, along with two other Manchester DJs, Jason Boardman and Elliot Eastwick, ran a club night called Yellow, and they had one simple rule: if any track they played cleared girls from the dancefloor, they'd never play it again. Herbie Hancock's seminal 'Rockit' failed the test, much to the disdain of whichever of them tested it out, but in the bin it went. The night was hugely popular, running every single week for seven years.

If the DJ following you is a known name and has hits of their own, never play any of their music in your warm-up set. You may convince yourself you're paying homage, but to them it's highly annoying and the height of bad manners. This is another reason to lay off the obvious big tunes of the moment, full stop; leave them for the next DJ. Far from passing up on a chance to steal the glory, you'll win a lot of friends this way - other DJs, managers, promoters and crowds never forget a good warm-up DJ. Get good at doing the above well, and doors to main-room peak-time sets will open for you.

So let's talk about peak-time sets. In a way, they're easier. The dancefloor is full. The boys are dancing now (safety in numbers, crowd mentality, and hey, the girls are all on the floor). Your job is to manage that energy, and the way you do that can be summed up in two words: tension and release.

Great DJs know that if they can build the dancefloor up to breaking point and then finally give the crowd what it wants, they'll keep everyone happy. This 'tension and release' happens within individual tracks (most big dance tracks build to some kind of anticipatory break, then a big full-on moment), but you can do it cyclically throughout a peak-time set, too.

Space out the huge tunes that you think everyone will love. Try and weave in equally energetic but less obvious tunes in the gaps. Experiment at least once in every set with something you're not sure people will like; you may be pleasantly surprised, and people will forgive you if you come back strongly. Even though it's peak-time, don't play at full pelt; always leave yourself somewhere to go and dial back regularly, giving at least some of your crowd a breather and a chance to head to the bar. Try and rotate people, too (the rule being that if the bar makes money, you get booked again, and anyway, no dancefloor is big enough to fit absolutely everybody on it). There is probably only one single point in any well-programmed night where you can really let rip and go for the jugular, so pick it wisely; after all, once you've hit your peak, where have you left yourself to go but down? Good DJs play just under full-on, always with a suggestion of something around the corner, always preserving some of the tension that keeps dancefloors electric.

How to play mobile gigs

Mobile sets - to remind you of our definition, gigs where you turn up with all the gear, lights, and everything else - call for true versatility from the DJ, because more than any other type of gig, mobile gigs come in all shapes and sizes. Like bar sets, you'll be playing all night. But like club sets, there will be dancing - although this may only be for an hour or two at the end. You may well start off playing a bar type set (many mobile DJs even have auto playlists for the start of events) as people eat food as part of the event, and only later will you be turning the lights on, the volume up and performing for the masses.

Despite the fact that mobile DJs are sometimes looked down on by the cool club guys and trendy bar and lounge jocks, playing mobile is hard to do well. Your audience can often be several generations deep, their tastes hard to predict, so the music will have to cover a lot of bases. It will always be commercial rather than niche, underground or trendy (remember a lot of these people do not come to places where music is played loud or dancing happens often). Mobile DJs have to carry big collections that cover several decades, and be ready for (and able to fend off tactfully) all types of requests. They often need to be diplomats as much as DJs, and while the cliché 'people person' can be used for just about any job where you have to interact with the public, it really is true for mobile jocks. Having a genuine empathy for everyone on your dancefloor is essential if you're going to play everything from the Beatles to Notorious B.I.G. and make it work.

The structure of a mobile DJ set will vary hugely depending on what the event is - a wedding is very different from an eighteenth birthday, for instance, and to an extent, the rules for club DJing as regards warming people up also hold true here - but a good additional rule when faced with a varied crowd is to play for the older people first (and the children if you're expected to entertain kids in the daytime section of your booking). Play for the more usual dancing crowd among your audience later when the majority of the older folk have had enough dancing or have left. An easy way of doing this is to play through the years in your collection, only bringing the music bang up to date for the final section of your show.

One calculation I always make when booked to play things like birthday parties is to work out the year when the oldest significant section of my expected crowd first went out dancing themselves, and bring music from then forwards. So if I'm playing a fortieth birthday, I'll take twenty-three years off the current year (going back to when most of the crowd were first going out themselves) and bring big hits and great dance music from that year forwards to today with me, basing most of my set around those songs. (Of course, you have to consider parents and grandparents if it's that type of event too, but you get the idea.)

Mobile DJing isn't about your mixing skills. Most mobile DJs don't really mix music, not least because many simply never learn - it's not in the remit. One thing they can and will be expected to do, though, is interact with their audience by talking on the microphone. Whether introducing the music as they move through the decades, basically as a mixing method (take a cue from radio DJs here: talking between every two or three tracks works), egging the crowd towards the dancefloor, conducting party games, or giving shout outs (think announcing birthdays, calling last drinks at the bar for the manager), using the microphone is inescapable for anyone who wants to play mobile gigs.

Indeed, using the microphone is something all DJs need to do at one time or another. I once saw a big festival-type DJ/producer, playing in front of tens of thousands of people, plug his headphones into the microphone socket on the mixer, something that took me full circle. It was a trick I first pulled when I was still at school: we'd forgotten a microphone for a charity gig I'd organised, and - much to the amusement of a local personality radio DJ who I'd booked as our guest - we had to conduct the entire gig mumbling into an old pair of Sennheisers. (Pro tip: this works fine. Plug 'em in and shout into one of the ear cups. Only one of them will work, though, so try them both…)

Whether you're shouting into your headphones, or – far more preferable – into a proper microphone (go for a wired dynamic mic), the trick is to lower the volume of the music when you're talking (often there will be a 'talkover' function on your gear to do this automatically for you). Hold the microphone close to your mouth and speak much more clearly and slowly than you'd normally feel comfortable doing, all the time avoiding the dreaded feedback, that piercing high-pitched noise that happens when a microphone is too near to a speaker that's amplifying it. (If you do struggle with feedback, turn down any monitor speakers near to you, turn them away from you, turn away from them, move the microphone closer to your mouth and turn *it* down, or try altering the mic EQ on the mixer.)

More than any other type of gig, mobile is where you're likely to be asked to play requests. Dealing with requests is often one of the hardest parts of DJing because ultimately you've been hired to know what music to play, not to be pushed around, playing what a vocal minority of people want. If you were to note down and find a way to play everything those few people asked you for, two things would happen: they would do it more, because they'd work out quickly that if they ask, they get, and your DJing would suck. You'd be a human jukebox playing ill-considered music that pleased fewer people than would have been the case if you had followed your training and instincts. It's a lose/lose.

That isn't to say you should be rude, or ignore requests. Remember, a big part of your job is to inject positive energy into the room, not be moody with the very people you are meant to be getting on side. While this is often an exercise in diplomacy ('Have you got something we can dance to?'; 'Can you play my track now, we're going in a bit?'; 'I've got it on my iPhone here! Surely you can plug it in and play it?'; 'Can you play something *good*?'), requests *will* be useful as they'll help you gauge what an unfamiliar crowd wants. The trick is to remember that they are just that: *requests*. And requests can be turned down. DJing is about programming, so don't let inappropriate requests throw you off your general plan for the event.

A good rule is to tell the person asking that you'll play the song a little later (if you intended to anyway - but feel free to make it look like it was their idea, they love that stuff). If you have a requested track and would consider playing it but you're not sure, 'I'll play it if I have time' works well. And if you don't want to play a track, or you don't have it, 'Hmmm, I'll see what I can do' or 'Sorry, not tonight' depending on the person in front of you can be appropriate.

In this step of the process you've learned all you need to know to make a success of your first public DJ gig. Hopefully you'll come out of the other side enthusiastic and ready for more. The next and final step of the process contains all the information you need to promote yourself successfully, turning that first gig into a string of gigs, whether you are aspiring to DJ occasionally, doing it as a part-time job, or even full time.

Step Five: Promoting Yourself

In this fifth and final step of the process, I'll show you how to build on your initial success as a DJ and turn it into something longer term. We'll cover the importance of playing out regularly, and I'll show you the types of DJ gigs you want (and don't want) to be aiming for. We'll deal with building a DJ profile and how to get involved in your local scene. I'll give you proven techniques for landing DJ gigs, and show you how to ask for (and get) money for playing them. We'll look at promoting your own parties and how to set yourself up as a mobile DJ. And finally, we'll cover how becoming not just a DJ, but a 'DJ/producer', has become a sure-fire way of achieving DJing success today.

Why You Need Regular DJ Gigs

Introduction

Really, when we say 'DJing success' we mean 'DJ gigs'. The skills of DJing can only be sharpened against the steel of the public. If you want to get better at knowing the right track for right now, you need people in front of you to give you the feedback that you improve from. If you want to know whether the transition you just performed bored or delighted, you need people in front of you to watch. If you want to build your confidence around knowing how to get your body language, behaviour and tone right to bring a cold room of strangers to a warm, welcoming mass of happy humanity…I think you get the idea. Without the humanity to feed off, it's a non-starter.

Not only that, but gigs lead to more gigs. One of the best ways to get booked is to be the one playing the tunes, because the people who hire DJs are often among the people you're DJing to. If you've ever looked from the outside and wondered how to break into a circle of a small number of DJs who are constantly getting all the work they can handle, one of the truths is that the circle is self-perpetuating. In other words, once you're in, you're in. Finally, never forget that gigs are fun. They're addictive. When you've had the real thing, there's no going back.

Once you're regularly DJing in public, you tend to find that people assume you can do all types of DJing. If you're bold and prepared to work hard at doing a good job of whatever comes your way, this can be a good thing. You may think you're an underground house DJ, but your workmate asks you to play her dad's birthday party, so you have to shuffle together a commercial set. At that party, it turns out one of your friend's dad's mates runs a local bar and needs a regular DJ for a Sunday daytime Ibiza-style chill-out gig. So you assemble your favourite B-sides and back-to-mine type tracks and take the gig – and end up loving it. And eventually, that bar residency leads to you being asked to fill in for an absent DJ warming up a local club. Suddenly, you're playing the underground house sound you love every week, and getting paid for it. Bingo! And it was being versatile that led you to where you wanted to be all along. Indeed, if a tiny bit of you says, 'I could do that' when you're offered a gig, even if the rest of you is screaming, 'No!', seriously consider taking a deep breath and going for it.

Types of gigs to go for

Private parties for family and friends are a traditional starting point for DJs. They are easy to get, and a good place to practise. On the downside, they are unpredictable, can be totally naff, and are hard work (you may need to bring all the gear, and then put up with constant harassment from people 'wanting a go' or trying to dictate the music). These types of gigs are hard to turn down, but it's best not to base your DJing dreams on landing a regular stream of them.

You may choose to advertise your services as a mobile or corporate DJ, playing company parties, birthdays, school events, and so on. It's easier than you might think to get set up to do this kind of event (we have a chapter on it coming up), and it's the best way of getting into a situation where paying work leads to more paying work, so if your personal definition of DJing success is 'paying gigs' rather than just 'gigs', this could be your best route. Or you may be lucky enough to land yourself a regular slot in your local club right from the off, although such gigs are extremely rare for new DJs. The competition is invariably fierce, and you need to know how to stand out to have any chance - or know the club owner. (There's actually a better way of getting club gigs, and we cover it in a coming chapter, too.)

Which leads on to bar gigs. Luckily, most of us live in or near enough to a town or city with at least a handful of half-decent bars, pubs or lounges where music is played. Getting a slot in such a venue is possibly your best chance of playing regularly when you're starting out, giving you the opportunity to practise your skills week in, week out, and play some semblance of the music that got you into all of this in the first place - even if it is to a half-empty pub on a Tuesday night. Such bookings are fantastic for getting you out of the domestic and into the real world in public, where the dynamic is completely different to spinning at parties for friends and family. You're on show, and despite the fact that you may often find yourself playing to a handful of people, you have a reliable, hopefully weekly, gig on which to build. Bar gigs are more attainable than club gigs, and they require less commitment as far as finances and organisation are concerned than setting up as a commercially available mobile DJ. And if you play for six months to a half-empty bar once a week, suddenly you've got twenty-five DJ gigs under your belt. Something will come of that, I can guarantee you.

There are only two types of gigs to put from your mind at this stage, one because if you mess it up you ruin someone's life, and the other because you're not going to get it.

The first of these is the wedding DJ booking. Wedding gigs involve far more than playing music. You are a compere, often an MC, taking charge of various aspects of the day and following a protocol that you need to understand to get right. You have a single chance to do so, and if you mess up, two people who have been looking forward to this day all of their lives are rightfully going to be livid with you. Weddings are for specialists who know what they're doing; they are not places to fake it till you make it. If you're interested in wedding DJing, befriending and shadowing a DJ who already does it, or at least getting some specialist training, is essential.

The second type of booking to forget about is the big festival-style gig, where you tour your country or continent, being put up on the big stage to play your hour of huge tracks in front of tens of thousands of adoring fans. The truth is that you're not going to get booked to play outside of your home city at all, never mind on the big stage, until you've done what I'm suggesting: taking small bar gigs and building up, honing your craft, and in many cases taking ten years to become an 'overnight success'. Another truth is that only when you've got music out there that you've produced yourself will people come to shows to hear you play.

Actually, making your own music is perfectly possible, and when you do, you'll have a huge advantage over many people who produce their own music and then get booked to DJ: you'll already know *how* to DJ. A good route to the festival stage, then, is to learn to DJ, learn to produce music next, then start gunning for such gigs when the agents who can get you them start knocking on your door, which will be when one of your self-produced tracks blows up.

So easy, tiger. In both of these cases, there's a path to be trodden first. He who gigs, wins, so at first, go for the gigs that aren't life or death, specifically those that you can actually get.

One thing that'll make it much easier to get any type of DJ gig is a decent online profile. That's what we'll look at in the next chapter.

Building Your DJ Profile

Introduction

'You are', goes the mantra of our times, 'what Google says you are.'

One of the things practically anybody who is interested in you as a DJ is going to do between finding out about you and asking you to play a DJ set in their bar, at their party, or in their club, is Google you. You need to own what they see. This chapter contains quick, easy tactics for doing that - tactics that anyone can put into practice, and that work.

The good news is that you can gain a real advantage here. Despite the competitive nature of DJing, many DJs are rubbish at maintaining an online presence, so by simply ticking the following boxes properly, you're giving yourself a tangible head start. But other more subtle things happen when you consciously craft a public profile or brand for yourself. You are forced to see yourself and your DJing more how the general public see it (this is a good thing, by the way), and you naturally begin to exercise some discipline over your DJing work ('I really must post a new mix on my website as promised this week...').

As well as making a good impression on anyone who could be in a position to offer you work, having an online profile does something else that's hugely important for you: it helps you to grow a fan base. A blunt fact of the DJ circuit is that DJs with fans get booked – or to put it another way, it doesn't matter how good you think you are, if you can't convince enough people to come along to see you when you DJ, the only time you'll show off how good you are is DJing in your bedroom.

Choosing a DJ name

Your DJ name may be your real name. If it sounds good, if it's easy to say, if it's distinctive enough to stand out, if people tend to write it down correctly when they hear it spoken (what I call the 'radio test'), and if you're happy to have your real name associated with your DJing (people who have serious day jobs might not be as they may need to be Googled for their real name as well as for their DJ name), then go for it. If not, you need to find something different.

Picking names is a time-honoured rite of passage for DJs, bands, actors, and anyone else with a public persona they want to separate from the name they were born with. From putting pins on dictionary pages to using online random name generators, from looking up how your name is spelled in other languages to changing a letter of two of your name until it sounds cooler, from simply adding 'DJ' before your existing name to adding something between your given name and surname to give it a fresh flavour, there are lots of things you can try. Just make sure to test any ideas you come up with on other people before committing to them. And nowadays, you can't only have a name; it has to be designed into a logo too for use on your site and promotional material. Use a designer friend, a site such as 99designs.com or fiverr.com, or search 'freelance logo design' on Google for other options, but only do it yourself if you know what you're doing.

How much time and effort you put into getting this right depends partly on your ambitions. If you want to be the next global superstar DJ, finding the perfect name and logo has more importance attached to it than if your ultimate goal is to become a great DJ and play a couple of times a year in your local town. Bear this in mind, and in the latter case, don't worry if you can't come up with the most amazing name ever for yourself. The main tests are listed above, so work through them, get lots of opinions, and you'll be fine.

But there is one more thing: you'll need to secure any name you choose for yourself online.

Ideally, you'll want the name you've chosen exactly as it is spelled, no dashes or additions, as a .com (.com is the best extension by far as it's the one people always try first), and on the most important few social networks in your country too, which for many people will be Facebook, Twitter and YouTube as a minimum. If not, variations are OK: using your country's web address ending instead of .com, adding 'DJ' to the end - whatever you can find.

Elements of an online profile

Once you've found a name, buy the web address you choose and register on your chosen social media services. On Facebook, you'll want a Facebook Page for your DJ name rather than using your personal profile, even if you choose to use your real name, as Facebook Pages are more flexible than personal profiles. You're going to need somewhere to host your DJ mixes online too, and again where you choose depends on where you are in the world and the popular services there; just be sure you choose a legal site that you're confident your mixes won't disappear from one day. Also, look for somewhere that has widgets available so you can include them on your web page and elsewhere, and let people listen to your mixes directly from your own website or social media platforms without having to go to the mix website itself. My recommendation for a service that ticks all of those boxes is Mixcloud.

Some DJs ask whether it's really that important to have their own website when they could just maintain, say, a Facebook Page for their DJing. It most definitely is. The thing about a website is that you own it. It is the centre of what you do, and it's highly unlikely anyone will ever take it away from you. While social media services may rise and fall, or you may fall in or out of favour with them (it's easy to get accidental copyright issues on YouTube, for instance, that can get your channel banned), as long as you have your own website at the heart of what you do, all won't be lost.

There's an even more important reason why you need a website: it allows you to gather email addresses from fans and potential customers. People have predicted the death of email for decades now, but it never happens. Email addresses are still the gold standard way of contacting people, and the more email addresses you have of fans and prospects, the better. We'll talk about how to use email addresses you've gathered in a minute, but first, let's cover how to get your website and email system set up.

Setting up a website

Your site needs to have very little on it to do the job you want. You need a short biography page (two paragraphs about you is fine - name, location, music styles, a few places you've played), a contact page (with or without a form - a clickable email address is fine, plus a phone number), testimonials if you can get them, a blog part where you can post regular updates (mixes, news of gigs you've played and so on), and some photos (both from gigs and press photos). Get photos done professionally if you can, and please, no wearing headphones in meadows - keep the DJ gear to the DJ booth. If you're busy enough, an 'upcoming events' calendar can work, but there's nothing worse than an empty one, so wait until the right time to add this.

If this all sounds difficult, the good news is that it's got much easier in recent years. Most of the world's sites like this run on a platform called WordPress, which is free and easy to get up and going. Other site-building services exist too, and a popular alternative is Wix, or the place you bought your web address from may offer a similar service. If you're not confident about doing it yourself, get a web-savvy friend to help you buy your domain name and web hosting, get your site building app installed, and find a theme that you like (themes are like the paint job on your site). Make sure the theme you pick is responsive (that means it looks good on 4-inch smartphones as well as on 27-inch desktops, and everything in between), slot your logo in top-left and you're nearly done. All that's left is to add email capture to gather fans' details.

You could add in a system where you request fans email you, then gather all the addresses up and cut and paste them into your email system manually whenever you want to let your fans know about a gig or new mix, but that's pretty inefficient and unprofessional. Nowadays, there are many services that specialise in helping you gather addresses for email newsletters, make nice looking newsletters and send them properly, and some such services give you basic packages for free. They'll have a way to make adding a form to your site easy, and once you've gathered a few addresses, you log in to their website and follow some simple steps to send to your list. One of the most popular is MailChimp, although many others exist, such as ConstantContact or AWeber – Google 'online email marketing solutions' to bring up a list.

Maintaining your online presence

Of course, once you've set all of this up, you need to do something with it. Grab a calendar and work out how much time you want to commit to maintaining your online presence, and stick to it. You may commit to doing a DJ mix once a month, posting it to your mix service then to Facebook and Twitter, as well as embedding it on your own site so people can listen from there. You may choose to post a five-minute video introducing where you are and carrying a bit of footage of you on the decks and of your dancefloor on YouTube each time you gig. You may decide to write up all your gigs with photos for your site, and each time get a testimonial to add to the testimonials page. And you may decide to email everyone on your email list once a month with links to things they may have missed (gig photos, mixes, news of where you'll be playing, and so on). Your schedule can change, of course, but setting it and sticking to it will ensure your carefully built online presence doesn't become a ghost town, and will help you to own your name on Google, which is the point of all of this. Remember, Google loves fresh content.

Finally, in order to grow your blog readers, social media followers, and email list, it's important to let your audience know about all of them. Cross-advertise between them (have your social media profiles on your site, link to Twitter from Facebook, and so on), have them listed in your email signature, but don't forget offline. A business card is essential, and a great place to feature your web and social media addresses alongside your phone number.

Getting coverage elsewhere

The final part of the online jigsaw is to reach beyond your own website and social media presence and get other people to feature you on their sites. The reason for this is that the first page of Google for any established DJ will consist not only of their own site, YouTube and so on, but also places where other people have written about them. Local papers and music websites are always hungry for people to write about, so make sure you keep them informed of what you're up to and anything about you that you think they may find newsworthy. Get to know the people who write for these publications via Twitter to get your foot in the door. And always supply photos as well as written information; people are more likely to publish if you save them having to source a picture, and you want to dominate Google Images as well as the main search results.

However, having a great online profile is only part of the game. You have to get off your bum and into your local scene before you can realistically expect to play any part in that scene. In the next chapter, we'll take a look at why this is so important, and how to go about it.

Getting Involved In Your Local Scene

Introduction

For every DJ playing in public and getting paid for it, there are scores of DJs wishing they had that person's job. Ever seen a DJ in a venue and thought, 'I could do better than that'? You probably could - but invariably what that DJ is doing better than you is the stuff you'll read about in this chapter. You could call it networking. I prefer to call it getting involved in your local scene. And make no mistake, this is important. Never was the cliché 'it's not what you know, it's who you know' more true than in the world of DJs.

It has always amazed me how many people expect to get DJ bookings yet never do any of the things we are about to look at. Instead, they think that if they put a DJ mix online or burn a few CDs and shove them in the hands of venue managers, the work will start coming in - as soon as people hear their mixes, they'll think, 'Wow, this is the DJ we've been looking for all this time!'

But it doesn't work like that. Nobody who can give you a gig has the time to listen to your DJ mixes to start with. Even if they do, they never base booking decisions on them. It would be like a jobseeker randomly giving out CVs and expecting offers of employment to come flooding back without bothering to find out if there were vacancies in the first place. Imagine a job market where vacancies are never advertised, and when one does come up, the employer invariably already knows the person they'll end up giving the job to. That's the opaque world of local DJ bookings. That's the world we've got to help you break into.

Doing your basic research

So let's see where you're at right now. How much do you know about the DJ scene in your local area? Have you visited all the venues that have DJs? Do you know what companies are behind the various pubs, bars, lounges and clubs? Do you know who actually books their entertainment? If you look at an event advertised in your town, can you guess who the promoter is? Is it a local person, or an out-of-town company? What about the DJs themselves: do you know which DJs are getting the work? If you're planning on playing mobile gigs, have you made a list of all the mobile DJ companies and worked out who the successful ones are?

Great DJs make it their business to know their local scene and everyone in it, both to become clear about what opportunities are there and to get to know the people who pull the strings. You can start this online (definitely following and getting involved with the social media activities of everyone and anyone in your town who's involved in your local scene), but ultimately, you're going to have to complete the job out and about.

Study your local what's on websites (and listings magazines, if they still exist), subscribe to promoters' newsletters, and keep a diary of what's going on in your town, then strategically get yourself out there. Yes, it might cost you a bit, but if you commit to getting your butt out of the door once or twice a week, you'll find ways of making it happen. Your aim is to go to every single venue in the city you want to play in that has, or you think might have, DJs, on all kinds of nights, quiet and busy. Throw in your attendance at charity events, local festivals, street parties and so on, and you'll be halfway there.

Getting to know people

If you're planning on being a mobile DJ, frankly you don't need to become a wall-fly of your local DJ scene as I've just discussed, although venue knowledge will still be useful, as will getting to know venue managers and other local mobile DJs. When it comes to expanding your presence, you can attend formal networking events (breakfast meetings and the like) and literally work the room, gathering and giving out business cards and practising your pitch.

But otherwise, if you're a DJ trying to break into what can appear to be a closed local scene in pubs, lounges, bars and clubs, getting out there is essential. Truth is, though, it's only half of the game. The other half is that you need to get to know people. Call it networking, being sociable, putting your face about, whatever – the sometimes uncomfortable fact is that you need to talk to people. Being there isn't enough.

So before I give you some suggestions, let's again see where you are now. Do any of the people we spoke about earlier, the movers and shakers in your local scene, know you? Are you on speaking terms with at least some venue owners, managers or senior bar staff? How many people who DJ in your local scene know who you are and what you do? Are there DJs in your circle of friends who will introduce you to people? How many local players have you managed to get connected to online, via forums, social media, and so on? Can you arrange to be in the same place as them, buy them a drink and have a chat?

Good networkers know they have something of value to give, but understand that they need to see everything from the perspective of the other person, humbly looking for ways to get involved and help out. You're never expecting anything in return, but you trust that if you give – and give for the right reasons – that is exactly what you'll get.

Luckily, you're already on the right path. You have something of value to offer (you've played at least a gig or two, have a nice online profile, and are working social media and starting to gather email addresses of your fans), so now you need some tactics for spreading the love in your local scene to get something in return when you've earned that right.

If you make it your job to call into the cool local beach bar that has DJs every evening when the place is quiet, and sit at the bar itself, you'll soon be friends with the bar staff, or even maybe the manager. If you haul yourself off the sofa on a wet Tuesday to go to an event you know is likely to be close to empty but is something you'd possibly enjoy, your attendance will be noticed, plus the chances are that anyone else there will be equally committed to the local scene and may well be worth knowing. If you arrive unfashionably early at a big all-day music festival in your town, again you may meet a few equally eager fans and even brush shoulders with some of the artists (with events that have large billings, often some of the performers will head out into the public areas to soak up the atmosphere early on).

There are other things you can do that are a bit more planned to give you the chance to meet people who may be able to help you in your DJing career. For instance, you could:

Volunteer for local charity events. If there are any charity events involving DJs, music, or your local clubs or venues, volunteer to help set them up and promote them. You could give our flyers, put up posters, distribute tickets to local shops, offer to run the VIP list on the night. Often these are organised by non-scene people (local councils, the charities themselves), but they can be a good 'in' as they will put you in contact directly with the DJs, venue managers and so on you ultimately want to befriend. Just help out for the right reasons: get genuine satisfaction from helping and trust that good things will come back to you, because they will.

Offer to review events for your local listings website or magazine. This can get you into gigs for free and give you an excuse to talk to DJs and other players, all of whom will hopefully appreciate your incisive words when they are published. If you're not confident about asking for work from other outlets, just blog about nights out on your own site. Be sure to tag the artists you write about to increase the chance that they'll see your work. Follow up on any reactions. Introduce yourself in person next time you see them…

Help out with club nights you admire. When newer promoters are setting up events, they are unlikely to turn down sincere offers of help. If somebody decides they want to start booking out-of-town DJs to promote a certain musical style or scene in your town that hasn't been done before, for instance, they'll often be committing a lot of their own money and time trying to make it work. If you can genuinely get involved and help out of respect and love of the music, you'll be received with open arms. Again, online promotion, flyering, offering to drive guest DJs to and from the airport…these things are not only invaluable, but of great use to you in getting involved and known among people who could eventually help you get DJ work.

Get a job in the scene. Back before digital music, the local record shops were tried and tested places to get to know everyone, but with their demise, you'll have to think more creatively. Bar staff are always needed in venues, or if you have any knowledge of lighting or sound engineering you could get yourself a job doing either thing in your local club (you then often stand next to the DJ in the booth all night). Or maybe there are promotion companies or DJ agencies in your city that have openings. You can do some of these jobs part-time if you work a day job.

Finding a mentor

A mentor is like a super contact, a holy grail person who can seriously speed up your progress as a DJ. In the mobile DJ scene, it's pretty easy to find a mentor because there are few mobile DJs who would say no to someone helping them to pack the gear, set it all up, and then break down at the end of the night – it's hard work. Land the job of being a mobile DJ's helper (and be honest about your intentions), and far from seeing you as competition, your mentor may well groom you either to take his or her place for the odd gig or to help out with double bookings and so on.

Mentors often find you rather than you finding them. They'll be someone who sees something in you that they remember from their own past; someone who wants to nurture you, but realises your ultimate potential to take their place – and they'll be cool with that. These kinds of people are going to become life-long friends, and you'll be forever indebted to yours if you find a good one.

I was lucky enough to have Dave Haslam, a key DJ at the famous Haçienda club in Manchester, as a mentor. He asked me to play a guest spot or two at a club night he ran, and our relationship grew from there – my DJ partner and I eventually ended up taking over his Saturday night slot. As much to give us the best chance of succeeding in our new role as anything else, Dave mentored us in promoting, marketing, building a fan base, offering something different, and dealing with the industry. Even now, decades later, I still count Dave as instrumental in getting me to where I am today.

There's no point trying to pay someone to mentor you, or forcing the role on anyone, even if you already know them. It'll happen naturally if there's a chemistry between the two of you, and the other person wants to help. It's certainly true, though, that the more you get out there and get to know people, the more likely such a person is to appear in your life. When you realise somebody is mentoring you, don't take advantage of it or take too much of their time. Use them wisely and fairly and be grateful, because their freely given help will be something you'll find irreplaceable.

So with your eye on the types of gigs that are realistic to go for, a decent online profile, some local networking done, and hopefully a contact or two to guide and mentor you, you're close to getting the regular DJing work you're dreaming of. In the next chapter, I'll show you how to close the deal.

Landing Regular Slots

Introduction

You probably won't believe me, but if you've done everything I've told you so far in this section, a regular DJ slot is not going to be hard to find and may even come to you without you doing anything. You have the right mentality towards the types of DJ gig you're prepared to take, you have a good online profile and are starting to build your own fan base, and not only do you have a knowledge of your local scene, but you're friends with some of the venue managers, local faces and other DJs. Everyone knows you're a DJ, so if there's a DJ needed, you've now manoeuvred yourself into a position where you may well be asked to do it.

You just need to know how to close the deal, or what to do and say when the deal comes knocking - and that's what this chapter is about.

Spotting the gigs

While sometimes the work may come to you (family member wants you to play their birthday party because 'you're a DJ', college tutor asks you to do the end-of-year party because you know where to hire equipment, another local DJ is off on holiday and asks if you'll fill in a bar slot for him while he's away), most of the time at first it'll be you doing the asking, especially if it's a regular slot you're looking for.

You may hit gold and through your contacts find out that a prime Saturday night club residency has become available and nobody else is in the frame, but in reality the chances are slim that this will happen. Stories abound about DJs not showing up to play a big club slot, and the desperate club owner scrambling around to find a replacement, only for an untried local DJ to step up and save the day, thereby winning the slot for ever more. But while this does indeed happen, you can't build your search for gigs on the assumption that it'll happen to you.

In fact, good DJ gigs are often the ones nobody else has thought of. Spotting opportunities will teach you to be entrepreneurial in your DJing, which is precisely the way to think in order to land more and better work consistently. Here are the two main types of gigs you could be approaching managers, promoters, and venue owners to get yourself playing at:

Places that don't usually have DJs. Modern DJing gear has made gigs like this much easier as you don't need a full DJ booth to play any more – just room for a DJ controller somewhere in a corner. Think beach bars, cocktail bars, trendy restaurants, art installations, pop-up exhibitions, cool clothes shops, in-between bands in a live music venue, skate parks, ice rinks, sports bars…

The idea is to find a venue or business where you can imagine yourself playing a certain type of music and adding to the overall vibe, and convince whoever has to be convinced that it's a good idea. This kind of gig is good because you can own it, you'll take the credit if it works (and trust me, nobody remembers gigs that don't work, so your reputation won't be tarnished for trying), and it will teach you to have a vision for how DJing could improve a space and know exactly what type of DJing to do to make that happen.

Places that have DJs, but not at the time you're proposing. Local bar has DJs on a Friday and Saturday, but not for the rest of the week? Tell them that Thursdays are the new Fridays and you've got a great idea for filling that night. (Hint: make sure you *have* got a good idea.) Live in a seasonal town that fills with tourists for the summer months? Suggest a 'Twelve Summer Sundays' season where you play the Sunday afternoon sundowner slot for people pouring into a local music bar from the beach. New live music venue opened across the street from an existing pub? Suggest you turn up early at the pub and play for an hour or so before the venue opens to draw in a pre-gig crowd (you could hook up with the promoter of the gig to offer cheaper tickets or guaranteed entry to anyone who buys a drink in the bar you're playing at first). New type of music breaking through that wouldn't suit a weekend slot just yet, but you know it is gathering a following in your town or city? Take the worst night in a good venue and champion that sound – if the stars move in your favour and you pull a crowd, it won't be long before you're elevated to a better night.

Start thinking along these lines and asking around. Even though I made my DJing name playing main room club music, I used these tactics myself to get there. I have conceived and played disco Fridays, chill-out Sundays, techno after-parties, indie sets at live music venues – it's all about spotting the gap, working out the kind of music that may work, and asking.

How to ask for work

Finding the right person to ask is the first trick, but hopefully, if you're involved in your local scene and you've done your research, that will be obvious to you by this point. Picking the right time to ask is the next one. While sometimes it works to make an appointment, often it's a conversation you can simply have at the venue, which means catching the manager there when he or she is relatively relaxed. Weekdays after opening but before the first rush of customers is a good bet for cafes, bars and so on.

Keep your conversation casual and show that you've done your research. There's no point pitching for a Wednesday night if Wednesday night is local band night (unless you're pitching to play between the bands, of course), and there's no point asking for a Monday slot, thinking you'll be more likely to land the worst night of the week, if Monday is the night the venue is shut. If you've done your background checks and think your idea is a good one (and maybe even discussed it with some of the bar staff or other DJs who work there), there's no reason why your pitch shouldn't fall favourably, as ultimately you have the interests of the venue at heart. Just remember to state clearly who you are, why it is you want to talk to the manager/owner, give them a short bit of your background, outline the problem ('Tuesday nights seem very quiet') and your solution ('I have an idea for a DJ night that should pull a new crowd'), explain your motivation for doing this ('I love the venue and feel we could build something good here'), and crucially, don't forget to get agreement on a clear next step ('Shall I call you tomorrow to get your decision? Is twelve OK? Let me check your number...').

While it's important to be sure of yourself, be aware that promising the world recklessly is silly; far better to outline your idea, set some boundaries ('Let's try it for four weeks and reassess when we see whether there's a market for it'), then follow through consistently and professionally.

The absolute wrong way to ask for work is to go in like some mad musical genius, mixtape in hand, pitching the revolutionary sub-genre you'll be playing, convinced that your amazing sets are going to change everything. As we learned earlier, venue managers want reliable, professional people who'll do the job with the minimum of fuss. Sure, they appreciate a bit of flair and good ideas, and of course they'll care about the music on one level, but if you want a gig working with *them*, you need to make it easy for them to work with *you*. This means being polite, business-like and showing an intimate understanding of the world of the person who has the power to say yes to you.

Getting paid

One of the most common questions DJs ask about money is how much to charge, but it's impossible to tell you that DJs get paid this, or DJs get paid that. It depends on the venue, the number of people through the door, whether there's a cover charge, the local DJ competition, whether the gig was your idea or you were asked, and of course where you are in the world. What is always true, though, is that if you bring value, you'll get paid more.

What I mean is not that you're doing the job well enough (hopefully if you've learned from half of what's in this book, you'll be doing the job better than most DJs in your town or city), but that you've done the work on building your profile, started to gather a fan base for yourself, researched where you're asking for the gig, and ultimately pitched a good idea to the person who matters. Get all these things right, and whether it's a free meal and some drinks in the local beach bar in return for a few hours of tunes on a Sunday afternoon, a little extra part-time income from your local club for an occasional warm-up slot, or a full-time job in a local resort, as soon as the person with the purse strings realises that your intentions are all about mutual benefit, you'll be in a good position to ask for what's reasonable.

Now, I wish I could tell you that the world of DJing is ruled by legally binding contracts, invoices, and smooth, hassle-free payments, but it's not. While DJs/producers who tour the world and are represented by agents tend to get paid this way, and people who work as mobile DJs, for entertainment companies, as full-time DJs in resorts or on cruise ships and so on have proper contracts or work as formal contractors, a lot of the more casual end of DJ work is paid for, well, casually.

The two issues here are legality and making sure you get paid.

Generally, you are required to declare any income at all from your DJing to the authorities, which means issuing an invoice for that payment, according to the laws of your jurisdiction. If you don't, you risk being caught, and – lacking any formal paperwork to start the conversation with – having a tax inspector decide how much they think you may have earned using any evidence they can find (internet searches, your name on flyers, evidence from your own website or social media, and so on). I once knew a DJ who was flying to a gig in another country and was stopped at the airport because the authorities thought he was trying to flee after years of not paying any tax at all on his DJ earnings. You don't want that to be you. Ask other DJs in your town what they do in order to get your local flavour on all of this, but a good rule of thumb is that as soon as your DJing rises above the odd one-off for fun, get an accountant's advice and go legit.

Just as stories of DJs not being completely honest about how much they've earned are rife, so are stories of DJs not being paid. Of course, there's no excuse for people not paying a DJ what they've promised to pay, but the nature of nightlife attracts characters who sometimes appear to have few scruples. If an event promoter hasn't made their money back on the night, they're going to look for corners to cut - and unfortunately, the roster of DJs they flippantly promised the earth to can be a tempting target.

While it's not always possible to take a deposit upon being booked, or to get payment before you start (both are good ideas if you can), finding the person who is going to be paying you immediately after you finish is paramount. If you wait until the end of the night, any one of a number of things could have happened, none of which work in your favour: the manager may have gone home, the promoter may have paid everyone else and got no money left, the person who booked you may be too drunk (or worse) to care any more about doing the right thing…

Always ask for *something*

In any activity which is glamorous, even though, on the face of it, it appears to be a job, there will be people willing to do it for free or for a cut price. DJing is no different. If you're honest, because you love the music so much, you probably feel the same, at least sometimes.

But while it's tempting to offer to play for free to get your hours on the clock, or to avoid the legalities or the hassle of getting paid we've just talked about, it does more harm than good. It undermines all the time, effort and money you've put into the craft, and it undermines all the other DJs who are insisting on charging for their services. Do charge, even if it's only a token amount. What it does for your sense of worth as a DJ, and the difference in how the person paying you will regard you compared to someone they didn't have to pay for, is profound.

Let me give you an example. Javier was a Spanish ex-national basketball player who owned a beachside bar in a Mediterranean town I once lived in. Due to its position, this bar got the best sunsets on the whole strip, yet his background music was poor. I convinced him to let me DJ on Sunday evenings for a token fee to see what we could build up. We added an outside mojito bar and got a nice little scene going, and I was making a small wage from it. Soon enough, other local DJs came out of the woodwork. One day, quite apologetically, Javier told me he was now booking other DJs. These guys had seen me playing Sundays, wanted to play his other weekend nights, and had offered to do it for free, assuming that's what I'd done too. They did a good enough job, so he was happy.

'Just so you know, though, you're the only DJ I'll ever pay!' he told me. Yet all I'd done was spot a need, offer to do a good job filling it, and put a price on it from the off. Always try to do the same.

There are exceptions, but not many. Private family events of course may well be done for love. Or, if you're suggesting a brand new idea to a venue manager who is prepared to give you a go to see if it works, you may offer to do the first night for free – but even in this case, it's still better to charge *something* for that first night. More importantly, the key thing here is to agree on the fee from the second week onwards, right there and then, so you know that when you're asked back, the payment conversation has already been had. And sometimes, DJs agree to play charity events for expenses, but I can think of no other situations when DJing for free is a good idea.

So-called 'pay to play' events, or events where you have to get rid of a certain number of tickets to get paid, are not a good thing. While it is absolutely your job to be worth employing, you are not the event's promoter, and there is a line to be drawn. Likewise, if a promoter promises you the earth, but says you'll be paid 'if we're busy enough', the chances are high that you won't be the one going home with any money that night. Use your instinct and avoid gigs where you think you'll end up playing for free.

Of course, you may actually *want* to be the promoter. Done right, promoting events pays much more than any individual DJ gets. And it's one way of guaranteeing yourself a DJ set, come what may. It was, indeed, the route I took that launched my professional DJing career. In the next chapter, I'll show you how it's done.

Throwing Your Own Event

Introduction

When I was sixteen, my school organised an entrepreneurial class where we all had to come up with a business idea. People made necklaces, printed T-shirts and mowed lawns, but my friend and I decided a better idea would be to start a lunchtime sweet shop in our school. Unsurprisingly, we did better than the rest – so well, in fact, that we ended up being told to shut down by the headmaster, only to cut him a deal on the profits so we could carry on…

And carry on we did, taking our handsome profits down to the local record shop every day and building a great collection of 7-inch and 12-inch singles, and eventually buying a battered old mobile DJ rig, complete with flashing rope lights. We were now, we decided, DJs, and would throw a party to celebrate.

The end of our school term was approaching. We'd become quite the celebrities at school through our popular sweet shop, which also gave us a handy place to sell tickets from, so we hired the local sports club's hall for the last Friday of term and had some tickets and photocopied posters made. On the night, we set our gear up (in the hatch between the club's kitchen and the main room), put a couple of girls from my class on the door to collect the money, and we were all set – our first ever event.

That was a long time ago, and honestly all I remember is the moment I filled the dancefloor playing my favourite tune at the time (New Order's 'Perfect Kiss'), and a fight in the toilets involving the next school along and a couple of broken toilet seats. Oh, and the profits. Yup, these things did well. Our little business was booming. And the best bit? We were playing our own music, all night long. We actually ended up throwing many such parties (including some for other schools, and eventually a big one for all the local schools in a real club).

Throwing your own events, I realised early on, is a great way to make more money and get more gigs than other DJs.

Fast forward to the world of today. Rather than being, in the words of Paul van Dyk, 'the geek in the corner playing records while everyone else has fun', we DJs are everywhere, meaning much more competition. Instead of needing access to a photocopier for posters and being able to afford the local printer for tickets, we've got the internet and social media and phone apps for free publicity, sales and ticketing – but everyone else has access to these resources too. Yet really, promoting hasn't changed much from what I just described, and the reasons it's worth doing haven't changed a bit: you get to throw a great party, you manufacture yourself a DJ slot at the same time, and you may make a bit of cash from it.

How to promote

Teaching you how to promote could fill a book by itself, so in this chapter I'm going to go through some important tips that I wish I'd been told rather than having to work them out for myself over the decades of promoting hundreds of parties, good, bad, full and empty.

1. Start small. It is better to play to twenty people in a venue that holds forty than to forty in a venue that holds 200. Really, you can't start too small. Keep everything - venue cost and size, promotional budget, number of guest DJs - small. If you fail (and you will, frequently), you'll 'fail small' too - meaning you'll find it easier to get up and do it all again. Probably the biggest mistake new promoters make is to think throwing money at an event to make a bang is the way to get success. It doesn't work that way - people go to what they know, so you need to spread the word about what you do by impressing half a dozen people at your first event, then a dozen, then twenty, and so on, building your credentials and audience slowly over time.

2. Pick a good night. Friday and Saturday are always good, but obviously harder to secure, unless you come up with a novel venue that doesn't usually do this kind of thing, which has risks of its own. One-offs around public holidays are good, because if everyone's off work on a holiday Monday, you can throw a Sunday night party and expect more success than any usual Sunday night. We were always fans of throwing parties on Maundy Thursday, the evening before Good Friday, because we figured we'd tempt people out a day earlier than normal and get their energy and money before anyone else.

3. Do it yourself. I was once handed a plum Saturday night weekly slot to promote, and promptly booked all the resident DJs from all the clubs in the area to be my guest DJs. I figured it'd make for a busy-looking flyer and get me involved with the local scene a bit more. Instead, it gave me a logistical headache, a load of mercenary jocks who didn't care about the success of my night, and an unfocused event that ultimately struggled.

'You're good enough to do this yourself,' my DJ mentor told me – and sure enough, a re-jigged event, with my DJing partner and me playing the music and one or two carefully selected guest DJs, solved the issues. It was really just a confidence thing.

Trust yourself to be able to DJ your own event – after all, that's why you're doing it, right?

4. Expect half the people to turn up who say they will. And frankly, that number is being generous. There's a phenomenon in the UK called 'Shy Tory Factor' which attempts to explain why so many people say they'll not vote for the right-wing Conservative (Tory) Party in elections, yet when it comes down to it, they do, throwing all the opinion polls out. There should be one called 'Shy Clubber Factor' too. It's a fact of promoting that just because someone says they'll come to your event (on Facebook, face-to-face, because they took a pile of free tickets), it really doesn't mean much at all. When the moment comes, many of them simply won't. I refer you back to point 1 - insure yourself thoroughly against this.

5. Build your night on a brand, not a music style. Come up with a name, a theme, a feel for your night, and do some basic branding, but don't try and brand your night around the music you're playing. If you base your night around the current trendy music genre, as soon as that genre is out of fashion (or you decide it isn't working for you and need to pivot), you're stuck. But a *brand* - well, that can evolve and move with the times. Plus, you may personally be obsessed with the twists and turns of every sub-genre of dance music out there, but your audience really isn't. Coming up with a club night brand rather than throwing a deep house night or whatever insures you against accidentally alienating a large proportion of your potential audience who either don't care or may even be put off by your chosen style.

6. Negotiate the right deal with the venue owner. Venue owners and managers will usually try and charge you for the venue, because if nobody turns up, they still make something. As a new promoter, you can't really argue against this, and it's a clever promoter indeed who manages to talk a venue manager into giving up a cut of the bar takings (I've never managed it in twenty-five years of promoting), so really the game here is to get that hire fee as low as possible. Point out that you're doing all the legwork, logistics and actual promotion, and these things cost time and money, then negotiate low to get the best outcome.

7. Use every trick you can to oversubscribe your event. It's an established fact of marketing that people only buy from those they know and trust, and bluntly, in promotion that means they either need to be your best friends (and even that often doesn't work – see point three) or you need to hit them hard and often with your message. That doesn't mean spamming their Facebook multiple times daily, though – that method fails because it is only one channel. Instead, you need to recognise that nowadays everybody is online all the time and everyone is offline all the time – so you need to use your own website, get other influential websites talking about the event (interviewing you, running competitions for tickets and so on), work social media, print posters and flyers (yes, still important), get on the local radio spreading your message, and tell everyone you meet. The best way to get guaranteed income is to sell advance tickets, so definitely push this option hard.

8. Collect email addresses on the night. The best promotional tool, even in this social media age, is still an email sent to someone who knows who you are and is happy to receive it. And one of the easiest things to talk yourself out of doing at your events is collecting email addresses from the small percentage of people who heard about your party and actually came. Make no mistake: these people are your solid gold super-fans, and even if they don't appear to be particularly enjoying themselves on the night, they are still far more likely to come again than anyone else. You simply have to stay in touch. Have a clipboard, iPad, whatever, promote some incentive for signing up (free tickets, free DJ mixes), and make damned sure you email them and let them know of your next party, without fail.

While promoting is undeniably a great way to give you a stream of gigs playing the music you love and meet your DJing heroes (because if you end up with a successful night, you'll have the funds to book them to play alongside you), it's a high-risk game that demands all your attention. If you just want to earn some extra cash from your DJing, there's another route, and it's one that 100 DJs follow for every single one who successfully promotes events. It is, of course, being a mobile DJ.

That's what the next chapter in this section is about.

Setting Up A Mobile DJ Business

Introduction

Like promoting your own events, setting up a mobile DJ business deserves its own book, and can turn into a full-time job. To recap what we mean by mobile DJing, we are referring to being a DJ for hire who has everything necessary to provide the music and lights for a party – have disco, will travel. As a mobile DJ you'll play Christmas parties, birthdays, children's events, weddings, retirements, church socials, civic ceremonies, and so on.

Many DJs successfully run such an operation either in addition to their nine-to-five job to earn extra money or alongside another musical endeavour, typically a club DJ residency or trying to break through as a music producer (see the final chapter). In the first case, mobile DJing provides a useful second income and something fun to do that can be very different from the day job, and in the second, mobile DJing provides a steadier, more reliable income than chasing dreams of DJ stardom.

Is mobile DJing for me?

It's common to hear wannabe club-style DJs dismiss mobile DJing as beneath them, not 'real DJing'. But considering the level of professionalism and knowledge needed just to maintain and use all the equipment properly, such comments do the craft of the mobile DJ a disservice. Mobile DJing is a skill in itself, and you'd be surprised how many famous DJs started their careers this way.

While DJing a church hall for an under-elevens crowd may not feel as glamorous as headlining a festival, there is still a right way and a wrong way to do it, and the DJ who takes the time to learn how to give people what they want in these situations sets him or herself up well for a career in front of more discerning and glamorous crowds. And anyway, to the rest of the world, petty distinctions between *this* type of DJ and *that* type of DJ mean nothing.

When a family member, or your boss, or the girl or boy next door says to you, 'Hey, you're a DJ, will you do my party for me? How much do you charge?', what are you going to say? You may find yourself agreeing to do it. That's how many DJs end up playing their first mobile event – they take on the challenge, find they quite enjoy it, and realise it slots in nicely alongside whatever else they do. For some, it turns into *all* they do. The truth is you're far more likely to earn an income, even a living, from this type of DJing than any other type (and if you become a good wedding DJ, for instance, you can easily earn in a weekend more than many DJs earn in a year).

Getting the equipment

A distinction between the mobile DJ and other types is that the mobile DJ is always required to bring all the gear with them - sound, lights, the lot. While you probably already own a controller or mixer and decks, generally you won't have a PA system or lighting rig at your disposal.

As we mentioned earlier, it is better to rent than to buy, at least at the beginning. When I started mobile DJing while still at school, my friend and I bought a very cheap DJ rig from an ad in the paper, but as soon as we were asked to play better venues, we looked up the local hire shop and started to rent equipment (our rig really wasn't up to much, it turned out). In renting, you avoid the commitment of spending money on something you may end up using only infrequently, you can usually afford to rent better equipment that you could afford to buy, and you get to try different rigs out to see what suits you.

Make sure you see a hired PA working, and that the company shows you how to set it up and break it down. Even better, see if they'll bring it to the premises and do that for you - you'll avoid the need to provide transport, and they may even agree to come and take it away again at the end. This is a godsend, especially at midnight when you're on your own.

Whether from your own possessions, the local hire shop, borrowing, or cobbling together from friends (and the classifieds...), here's the essential stuff you'll need:

A DJ controller/laptop/CDJ set-up. Whatever you usually DJ on at home will almost definitely be fine here, so don't stress about whether it's good enough for mobile. If your DJ set-up embarrasses you in public (but you know you can use it well), get a flight case and DJ with it inside - instant pro look for even the cheapest controller.

A PA system. The most important of your hire shop requirements. The headline figure here is how loud it is, which is measured in Watts, shortened to W, so 500W is a 500 Watt PA system. A good rule of thumb is five watts per person, so very roughly a closed 100-person venue needs a 500W PA system. (Open air and the bets are off - start exponentially adding power depending on variables as wide as the size of the open space and the predicted wind on the day.) Good PA systems tend to have floor-standing bass speakers and separate units for mid and high frequencies which go on poles or tripods. Size matters - there is no such thing as a small, loud PA system. It's physics.

Lighting. Lighting comes in two types - mood lighting and moving lighting. The former is usually used to make walls, the DJ booth and stages look more interesting, the latter is aimed at the dancefloor to add some visual dynamics and encourage people to dance. Modern lighting is lightweight, powerful and reliable, and has features such as sound-to-light (so you don't need a traditional lighting controller to get the lights in sync with the music) and remote control. Strobes, lasers, smoke and more can be hired or bought at a fraction of the cost of a decade or so back.

You'll also need the correct stands and trusses.

A DJ booth, console or stand. True, you could hope the venue can lend you a table. But from the point of view of looking professional and saving your back from stooping for hours over a too-low table, a DJ stand that you bring yourself to assemble and break down is preferable. You'll need to think about its facade, too, and many DJs take black sheets plus some kind of front piece to tidy up their set-up once it's all cabled up and ready to go.

A microphone. A dynamic mic, sturdy and with the correct lead to plug in to your equipment.

Tools, casing and accessories. Things like heavy duty gaffer tape for making trailing wires safe, flight casing to move all the gear around safely, decent extension cables, and both enough tools and the knowledge of how to use them to make quick repairs to all of this stuff as required.

In addition to the above, many mobile DJs carry a separate audio mixer to sit between their DJ gear and the PA where they plug in their microphone and a back-up music source, although you may be able to get away with plugging these in through your existing DJ gear. Having a separate mixer gives you the chance to tweak the EQ of the room separately from your DJ controller or mixer. Whether or not you go down this route will depend on how flexible your DJ set-up's inputs and outputs are, and what kind of inputs and control your PA system gives you.

Finally, you really do need a back-up system – a small extra DJ controller, a spare laptop, a CD player, a DJ app on your iPad, whatever. It's all down to you at mobile gigs, so being prepared is essential.

The business side of mobile DJing

If you hire yourself out as a mobile DJ, you are most definitely in the DJ business, unlike maybe playing a couple of hours in a local bar every now and then where things may be a bit looser. As such, you need to make sure you do what's relevant to you out of the following to protect yourself and your audiences, and to be able to command the right fees for what you do:

Register your business. Depending on where you live, there will be rules you need to follow to trade legally, and you'll have to follow the right business and tax laws as well as probably registering the name of your business. Get the advice of an accountant.

Obtain any required public performance licences. Again, this will depend on where you live. Venues often have to have licences, which may cover you, but mobile DJs get asked to play in all sorts of places, and you may need some kind of licensing anyway.

Obtain sufficient insurance. It's unlikely your home insurance will extend to covering your DJing endeavours, and venues often require proof of personal liability insurance before they'll let you play. Luckily there are specialist companies who offer both property and personal liability insurance for DJs.

Get a contract template. You'll need a contract template that you understand and know how to use, which you can then fill in and get signed off by anybody who books you. Not only does this look professional, but it is essential to make it clear to your clients (and to remind you) what you are and aren't providing, and at what cost. It gives you something to use in the case of any dispute over payment (if you're asked to carry on playing, for instance, past a set time, your fees will be outlined clearly here).

Join a DJ association. Professional associations tap you in to an immense source of experience, and can offer you discounts on DJ insurance, access to contract templates, and periodicals that will help you stay up to speed and educate you properly on the industry. Attending their events will help you network with other DJs and industry professionals, and as an added bonus, being able to put their logo on your website will tell the world that you're a professional - especially if they have a code of conduct you can sign up to.

Advertising your services

In addition to the things we've covered already in this section of the book, mobile DJs have several other ways to help them bring in the work. As mobile DJing is a recognised service and there is existing demand for it, it's less about hustling for work and more about making sure that when people are looking for you, they can find you.

Advertising your business annually in local listings magazines, websites and directories is a good idea. Printing posters or cards that can be displayed in workplaces and local shops is always worth doing. Over time, establishing relationships with local hotel managers, wedding shops, event planners, schools and large local businesses can make you their go-to DJ. (Hint: when it comes to businesses, make friends with the people who run the HR departments. They tend to be the people who get lumped with organising office parties.)

As long as your website is good, you're using social media properly, and when you play, you're doing a great job (word of mouth and recommendation are still the most important promotional tools you have), over time these steps will ensure that whatever part mobile DJing is to play in your overall DJing career, you'll get the gigs you're looking for.

One characteristic of those gigs, though – along with all the other gigs you're likely to get as a result of following what's been written in this book so far, of all types – is that those gigs will be local to you. But if your dream is to DJ around the world, and you're prepared to do whatever it takes to get there, there is another route. It's that route that we turn to for the final chapter of this book.

Becoming A DJ/Producer

Introduction

I've mentioned a couple of times that a sure-fire way to promote yourself as a DJ is to produce your own music. I've left a discussion of this route to stardom right to the end for two reasons. On the one hand, good DJs don't always make good producers, and I don't ever want you to think that because you're not interested or talented as a producer, that it precludes your becoming a great DJ. And on the other, just because you've produced a great track, that doesn't mean you are automatically going to be able to go out there and be able to DJ. The two skills are complementary, sure, but both deserve respect in their own right - and clearly, this is a book about DJing, not producing.

All that said, many new DJs aspire to be DJ/producers, and as with DJing, digital has lowered the barriers of entry into the world of music production considerably, to the point where nowadays you can make a track on your phone, never mind on a tablet or laptop. As you'll see too, producing music needn't be hard and doesn't necessarily need musical training or the ability to play an instrument. So if it's something you're interested in, read on for lots of ideas and advice on how to get started.

Why be a DJ/producer?

The hard truth is, if you want to become famous, play outside your own town, tour the world, get added to big festival billings, and live the full-on 'DJ lifestyle', nowadays you have to be able to produce music. Just one single hit can utterly transform your DJing prospects, attracting press coverage, agents, managers, and those elusive far-flung DJ bookings.

But it's not just about fame and success. DJs are creative by nature, and producing music is just an extension of playing it. After all, you have a head full of musical ideas, and producing music lets you get those out of your head and share them with others. So producing music can be an awful lot of fun in and of itself.

Finally, who knows what works and what doesn't work on dancefloors better than DJs? You already have a good understanding of song structure and arrangement, and of course, as music is your 'currency', you listen to a wide range of it as part of what you do day-to-day, giving you more ideas to draw from in your own productions. For all of these reasons, it's well worth having a go at making your own music. As you're about to see, it really needn't be as daunting a thing as you might think.

How to start making music

Realise that making your own music is not an 'all or nothing' affair. Instead, it's a sliding scale. The first step is arguably simply live remixing - chopping up tracks as you DJ to do something more creative than just moving from one track to the next. You probably already do this to an extent in your performances.

The next is simply doing this ahead of time, through taking someone else's track and editing it to make your own version (or 're-edit') to use in your sets. Using free software such as Audacity (PC/Mac), you can extend track intros and outros, edit out breaks, add effects, and basically make versions of things that better suit you. From here it's a small step to making 'mashups', where you take two or more tracks by other people and creatively blend them into something new. (Software such as Mixed In Key Mashup makes this easy for you by automatically matching the BPMs and musical keys of your source material to help it all sound good.)

From here we move into making tunes 'proper', but again, our sliding scale is in full operation. It is not only possible but common for producers to make tunes from commercially available 'sample packs', and many do, with great success. Sample packs are sets of sounds you can buy in order to assemble your own tunes, a bit like using Lego bricks to build a model house. They are professionally produced, sound great, are often provided in the same musical key so you don't have to worry about them matching when you put them together. Using modern, DJ-friendly production software like Ableton Live, DJ/producers can quickly sketch out ideas and piece them together to make tracks in this way.

Once you're comfortable doing this, the next step is to start adding your own compositions to your tracks, by playing melodies, basslines and so on. Again, there is much help available. To start with, many great sounds come packaged with production software, and you use these supplied sounds ('presets') to make your melodies sound great. Also, there are tools to tell you which notes will and won't work in the musical key you're composing in, making it easy for those who don't understand musical theory but have lots of great ideas to make tracks that sound good. And you don't really have to 'play' anything in the sense that a musician would understand, because you can take as long as you like to program your melodies in, and when you hit 'play' on your software, everything plays back in real time.

I'm not pretending music production is all quick and simple, because beyond this we can go as deep as you like - you can start crafting your own sounds (called 'sound design'), you can indeed record elements played live and add them to your tracks (drums, guitar, piano, whatever), you can sing or work with vocalists… but what I'm telling you is that you absolutely don't have to do this from the start, and many successful DJ/producers never do an awful lot of this more involved stuff at all.

The important thing is to do what sounds good to you with the skills and tools you have, set deadlines, play the results at your DJ gigs (there's another advantage of being a DJ/producer rather than just a producer: you can test your stuff in public), share your efforts with the world on services such as SoundCloud - and keep doing it. Your hundredth effort may be the one that gets you recognised - but that just means when you do break through, your new global fan base has 100 tracks you've already made to enjoy. Such are 'overnight successes' made.

Three myths about producing music

If you're not already convinced to have a go, here are some excuses we hear regularly at Digital DJ Tips from people who secretly know they want to produce but are still resisting. Hopefully they'll answer some of your questions and encourage you to start.

'You need lots of expensive hardware, and preferably a recording studio...'

This simply isn't true nowadays. As I said in the introduction, you can make music on your laptop, tablet, even your phone... and you don't need anything else other than your choice music production software (we recommend Ableton Live). You may want to add a small piece of hardware at some point, such as a keyboard or pad controller, but these are strictly optional. And the days of heading into the studio to even be able to record tracks are long gone.

'You need to be able to play a musical instrument.'

No. While understanding a bit about music theory (scales, chords, harmony and so on) will definitely help you, even that isn't essential as long as you have a good ear for what works and what doesn't on the dancefloor. You certainly don't need to be able to playing an instrument to come up with your own tunes and include them in your tracks, as so many of today's tools guide you through doing this. There's no need to play stuff in 'real time', and you definitely don't need to be able to read music. Work on all of these things, by all means, as they'll make you a better producer - but don't let the lack of any (or all) of them stop you starting.

'You need the help of professionals, such as "real" musicians, music producers and mastering engineers, to make tracks that are any good.'

As a modern music maker, you do all the jobs that a team used to do to make a track yourself. You are the band, to start with, taking care of the drums, bass, melodies and so on in your tracks as you program your tune, and you also 'produce' your own track, in the sense of making your ideas sound good in your software, which replaces another traditional studio job. You can even buy *a cappella* vocals so you can add vocals to your tracks without enlisting a singer.

There is a conversation to be had about mastering engineers. In the old days, mastering engineers took a finished track and hung around when it was being pressed to vinyl, tweaking the controls to make sure that the vinyl sounded as crisp, loud and amazing as possible. While big hits today are still 'mastered' in this way (although usually not to be pressed to vinyl any more), there's an alternative for bedroom producers to get at least some of that 'finished sheen' on their own tracks, in the shape of online mastering services. For a small fee, these services will let you upload your track, apply some proprietary magic to it, and download a polished version of it to release to the world. It's not quite the same, but it's a good start. Take a look at LANDR (www.landr.com) to see one such service.

All this said, please don't think that producing music is a simple gateway to DJing fame. Having both skills is not easy. It's also a competitive world out there, and just because you do it, it doesn't mean you'll automatically succeed at it.

Instead, do it because you decide that, just like DJing itself, it's something you're driven to do and that you feel will make you a more creative and fulfilled artist. And if you think you want to give production a go, don't wait to become a great DJ before you try and become a producer. Enjoy making re-edits and mashups, and having the odd go at your own tunes right from the off. Keep improving your knowledge and making more involved tracks, and keep testing your results on your dancefloors. If you do, there's no reason why it can't be you DJing headline slots at festivals in far-off places in the years to come.

Conclusion

My hope is that this book has given you the confidence to go out and play the music you love in public on your journey to becoming a great DJ. I hope it has given you enough knowledge to choose a DJ set-up that's right for you, offered enough guidance to help you craft a truly special music collection, and shown you all the techniques you need to start playing out. I believe that it's in public where DJing is learned, and that too many DJs give up before they get the rush of playing a gig in front of a real crowd.

If you take one thing from this book, let it be this: your only job as a beginner or bedroom DJ is to play out. Once you have done so, you've crossed the threshold and are ready to take your DJing in any direction you want. Hopefully the information in the final two steps of the process has given you plenty of tactics and ideas for you to go ahead and do just that.

I want to end by stating that DJing is a journey, not a destination, so always strive to be learning, whether it's about new gear, music or techniques, or about how to perform better or promote yourself more effectively.

So whichever direction your DJing takes you in, on behalf of all of the team at Digital DJ Tips and myself, I wish you the very best of luck. Now get out there and rock the dancefloor!

Acknowledgements

This book wouldn't have been possible without the help and support of the following:

My wife, Faye Morse.

Steve Canueto, Joey Santos, Lindsay Cessford, Lauren Andio, Philip 'Wozza' Worrell, Terry 42, Chuck van Eekelen and the rest of the team at Digital DJ Tips.

Terry Pointon, Dave Haslam, Constantin Köhncke, Dan Bewick, David Dunne, Alex Moschopoulis, Simon Halstead, Terry Weerasinghe, Yakov Vorobyev, Karl Detken and Baptiste Grange, for your advice and friendship over the years.

Lucy McCarraher, Joe Gregory, Alison Jack and the rest of the team at Rethink Press, without whom this book would be far less polished.

My friends at Pioneer DJ, Serato, Native Instruments, inMusic, Reloop, Allen & Heath, Algoriddim, American DJ, Chauvet, Promo Only, Atomix, Beatport, Focusrite Novation, Mixed in Key, Magma, Gibson Pro Audio and all the other amazing DJ, music production and pro audio brands I have the pleasure to work with.

Thank you to everyone named, and apologies to those whom I may have missed.

The Author

Phil Morse is a DJ who has played all types of gigs, from mobile to bars, radio, clubs and festivals, in a career spanning over twenty-five years. He held a guest residency at U2's Kitchen nightclub in Dublin, played at the world's biggest club (Privilege in Ibiza), and has DJed as far afield as Cuba as well as hundreds of times at his club residency at Tangled in Manchester, which ran for over fifteen years.

Starting out as a vinyl DJ, he was one of the first to adopt digital DJing back in 2004, writing about it for *iDJ* magazine in the UK. In 2010, he founded Digital DJ Tips, now the world's leading online school for DJs with over 13,000 students in fifty countries. Digital DJ Tips' courses teach everything from DJing basics through to music production, scratching, making mixtapes, and forging a career as a professional DJ.

He now lives in the Mediterranean with his young family where he still DJs, primarily at beach bars, corporate events and private parties.

About Digital DJ Tips

Digital DJ Tips exists to help people become great DJs, whether they're complete beginners, bedroom DJs, semi-pro, or returning to the game after a break, and whether they want to become club, party, mobile, radio or 'just for fun' DJs.

Find out more about Digital DJ Tips' DJ courses here: http://www.digitaldjtips.com/courses

Join Digital DJ Tips and get exclusive DJ news, training and offers for free here: http://www.digitaldjtips.com/join

Find out where you are in your DJing today, and get a personalised plan for improving your DJing for free by taking the Digital DJ Tips' DJ Test here: http://www.digitaldjtips.com/test

Follow Digital DJ Tips here:
http://www.facebook.com/digitaldjtips
http://www.twitter.com/digitaldjtips
http://www.youtube.com/digitaldjtips

Printed in Great Britain
by Amazon

86302246R00167